Oak Island
1632

Oak Island
1632

Written and published by
James A. McQuiston, FSA Scot
jamesamcquiston@gmail.com

The true mystery of the world is the visible, not the invisible.

– Oscar Wilde

TABLE OF CONTENTS

PREFACE

Early in 2017, I published a book called *Oak Island Missing Links*. In this book I explained how a number of trips could have, and probably were made to North America from the British Isles and the Nordic countries, before the voyage of Columbus.

I also explained how legends have sometimes taken many centuries to verify.

I presented my theories as to what the Mi'kmaq First Nation legends of Glooscap and Malsum might really represent, and what was being referred to in the *Zeno Narrative* by the words Zichmini and Estotiland.

These theories revolved around a potential voyage by Sir Henry Sinclair to North America, in 1398.

In *Oak Island 1632*, I focus for the most part on my theory that a group of Scottish settlers, being forced out of Nova Scotia through an Anglo/French treaty, may well have ended up on Oak Island, Nova Scotia, in the spring of 1632, leaving behind items that have become the focus of over 220 years of treasure hunting.

I explain the lead up to this event, and also the tragic aftermath that affected the principals involved in this Scottish settlement, along with the potential involvement of the Freemasons.

I also present logical solutions to many mysteries concerning Oak Island.

Perhaps most importantly, I make the case that the nine levels of the Oak Island Money Pit (similar to the nine levels involved in the Masonic ritual of the Royal Arch Degree) were not inspired *by* this Freemasonry ritual, but were possibly an inspiration *for* this nine-levels ritual, and also the likely inspiration for many Freemasons, over the last two centuries, taking an inordinate interest in Oak Island, as treasure hunters, investor, and as visitors.

The prolific Nova Scotian author Mark Finnan was first to draw explicit attention to the links between Freemasonry and the Oak Island legend. Finnan, in the 1997 edition of his book *Oak Island Secrets*, noted that many of the Oak Island treasure seekers have been Freemasons, and implied that the Masonic Fraternity possessed secret knowledge of the nature of the treasure, which compelled them to seek it. I'm inclined to agree.

It has been my extreme pleasure to work with the current owners of Oak Island and their staff in unfolding this mystery. I thank them for their interest and their encouragement to write my theories down in the form of this book, and my earlier book.

I also thank them for the wonderful, personal tour of Oak Island in June of 2017.

Most importantly, I thank them for vetting this book.

Just as my first book was vetted by two Scottish historians, *Oak Island 1632* has been vetted by Oak Island historians, who have found no historical errors.

Mine has been a sincere effort to use my decades of experience researching and writing about Scottish history to help satisfy my own lifelong curiosity about Oak Island.

It has been an immeasurable joy to share my findings with both the Oak Island searchers and researchers, and with those members of the general public who share this same curiosity.

While I may not have all the answers yet, I do provide some amazing information and evidence that has lain somewhat hidden until now, much like the treasures of Oak Island.

I welcome any comments. You may email me at: jamesamcquiston@gmail.com

Chapter One

THE ROAD TO OAK ISLAND

I first began my journey into the world of Oak Island research when, as I was updating a family history book, I remembered that my extended family held the premier Baronet of Nova Scotia title. This rang a bell as I eagerly watched an episode of the *Curse of Oak Island* TV show.

I wondered if the current owners even knew about the Baronets, who were first chartered in 1625, and who were sold land grants in Nova Scotia by a man who had been given that entire province in order to create a New Scotland there, just four years earlier.

It was in the original 1621 charter for Nova Scotia, granted to Sir William Alexander, that the name Nova Scotia was first used to represent New Scotland, as this is its meaning in Latin.

Although Alexander's settlement ultimately failed, the name Nova Scotia stuck, and the land did become quite heavily settled by Scots in the ensuing centuries.

It can at least be said that Alexander paved the way, and at a very high cost to himself and his family.

This is the story I aim to tell with this book, and it is all based on recorded Scottish and Nova Scotian history. It is not a wild theory or a mystical guess, but rather a credible answer to what happened on Oak Island.

Where it all began is hard to pinpoint, however our main character in this story launched his career by becoming a tutor of nobility. William Alexander's first known student was Archibald Campbell, the young Chief of Clan Campbell, and a kinsman to Alexander.

The name Archibald has a Gaelic version often written as Gylascop. It is my theory that an earlier Gylascop Campbell was the inspiration for the Mi'kmaq legend of Glooscap. The similarity in the names is at once obvious, but there are a few other reasons to believe this theory, which I explain in my book *Oak Island Missing Links*.

I don't intend to revisit my earlier theories about Gylascop and Sir Henry Sinclair in this book, although I believe it is possible that Sinclair set certain Scottish families on a course to create a New Scotland, and I explain my reasoning at length in my earlier book.

If Sinclair did, in fact, sail west, in 1398, to find a New Scotland, there can be no doubt that he had his reasons for doing so.

From 1378 through 1417, three men claimed to be the true Pope. With the Catholic religion being the only religion around (in the British Isles of that time) it can be imagined how this would shake everyone's faith in the church to have three men claiming to be Pope.

Also, the Black Death hit the British Isles in 1370, followed by three more plagues in a row, up until 1401. The Black Death claimed two out of every three people, killing an estimated 450 million people across Eurasia and over 200 million in Europe. It can be imagined how this would shake everyone's faith in science and medicine.

From 1384 through 1406, four kings ruled Scotland, along with a man who ruled it as a regent, refusing to ransom the rightful king. It can be imagined how this would shake everyone's faith in government.

Beyond Scotland, but still affecting its commerce and stability, the Hundred Years War was taking place between England and France, from 1337 through 1453.

Also, extending nearly to the Scottish border with England, a Peasant's Revolt took place in England, in 1381. Because of the general deterioration of life in Europe, peasants were beginning to revolt against nobility, which could potentially threaten the lifestyle of people like Henry Sinclair and other Scottish noblemen.

Adding to all of this drama and trauma was the dissolution of the Knights Templar, who once owned 640 properties in Scotland, including tenement buildings, churches, and homes, and who had connections to many Scottish clans. In Scotland, the Templars were well thought of and yet, because of religious and political pressure, individual Templars were forced to disappear into other organizations, or return to their parent clans.

Still, this was not all that afflicted Sinclair's Scotland.

Deforestation and depletion of resources were making life much harder for the average Scot. Through years of building ships, lodging, and fires for warmth, Scotland's once grand forests were disappearing. Also, minerals such as gold, silver, lead, and talc had been stripped from the land, at least as far as the easy-pickings were concerned. Even coal, as with wood, was being replaced by hand dug peat as the main heating/cooking fuel.

Generally speaking, life was just plain miserable in Scotland, in and around the year 1398. This helped lead to many inter-clan battles, as diminishing resources and land were fought over and clan feuds took root, especially across the Highlands.

Sir Henry Sinclair, and other noblemen who are said to have gone with him, would have had just about every reason in the world to want to secretly establish a New Scotland in a land to the west that he may have heard about through his Viking ancestors' sagas, or from other mariners, during his many trips sailing out into the North Atlantic to visit nearby islands.

I believe that, if they went at all, they went simply as explorers trying to lay to rest the Viking legends of Vinland, and to see if this new land to the west would be a good place to settle their families. This very settlement was attempted by Sir William Alexander, 230 years later, under the Baronets of Nova Scotia banner.

What is important about William Alexander and his student, Gylascop Campbell, is that the Campbell family was likely well aware of a land to the west through local legends and through the part of their bloodline harking back to the Vikings. William may well have heard these stories, too, as he descended from Clan Donald, which had a fair amount of Viking blood in their background, and were a great seafaring family in their own right.

Both men, being young and adventurous, and living shortly after the *Zeno Narrative* was published, may have had their minds filled with ideas of adventure in a New World across the North Atlantic.

In fact, these two young men visited Italy together, which is the land where the *Zeno Narrative* was published, and they visited within a generation of its publishing.

For those new to this story, the *Zeno Narrative* was a book published in 1558, in Venice, Italy, by Nicolo Zeno. It was said to be based on letters that earlier Zeno brothers had written to each other as far back as the 1398 voyage of Henry Sinclair to North America.

Looking at the book in hindsight it is easy to find errors in mapping and descriptions. But if one were to approach it from the point of view that very few people had any knowledge of the North Atlantic at the time, the book becomes much more believable.

This is especially true when you consider that a map published in the *Zeno Narrative* turned out, despite its errors, to be one of the most accurate maps of the North Atlantic from that period, and was relied upon by many seafarers for years, until better maps were drawn.

Add to this the fact that the author of the *Zeno Narrative* was already well known as a writer, and that his family had a long and distinguished history in Venice, and it seems less likely that he would have published a fraudulent story.

The book has its detractors as well as its supporters, but taken at face value, it appears to talk about a Scottish prince (presumably Henry Sinclair) for whom the earlier Zeno brothers served as navigators – in one case during a trip to a land that sounds much like North America.

Again, the Henry Sinclair voyage, and the veracity of the *Zeno Narrative*, are not central to my current story.

But it may well have been this book, and their own knowledge of a special land to the west, that excited Gylascop Campbell and his tutor, William Alexander.

A significant event in the life of William Alexander took place when Gylascop Campbell introduced him to the King of Scotland, James VI, who would soon become James I of England and Ireland as well. Alexander then became the tutor and gentleman usher (similar to the position of butler) to the son of James, who would one day take the throne as King Charles I, ruling the same kingdom that his father had ruled before him.

William Alexander would go on to serve in many government positions for King James I and his son King Charles I, along with becoming a substantial author of poems and plays. He has been called the unofficial "philosophical poet" for King James.

James was the only son of the famous Mary, Queen of Scots. When her cousin Elizabeth I, of England, died childless, James became the heir to the English throne.

For the first time in their warring histories the lands of Scotland and England (along with Ireland) were now happily represented by one king. This event caused the very birth of Great Britain. It took awhile for that name to catch on, although it was used in the court of King James from the time that he gained the throne.

What this meant, on a larger scale, is that, with the petty differences of these countries being set aside, new adventures could be carried on around the world. And thus, the global British Empire also had its beginnings in this single succession to the throne of Great Britain.

Add to this the fact that James I was responsible for the translation and printing of the *King James Bible*, a book that revolutionized the learning and use of words by the common man, and it is easy to see that the advancement of James Stuart to the kingship of England, Ireland, and Scotland represented a sea change in the history of the western world.

The significance of the reign of King James I cannot be overstated, and it was this very same King James who granted a charter to William Alexander for the land that we now know of as Nova Scotia.

Until this book, *Oak Island 1632*, it has remained somewhat of a mystery as to why James would choose to give away such a large chunk of the New World specifically to William Alexander. I'll explain soon.

James I knighted Alexander in 1609, and appointed him the "Master of Requests" for Scotland in 1614 – effectively the king's private secretary. In 1615, Alexander was made a member of the King's Privy Council.

The Privy Council was a small group of advisors to the king, much like the presidential cabinet in the United States, or the prime minister's cabinet in Canada.

Also serving on the Privy Council of King James I was Sir Francis Bacon, a man who has been connected to Oak Island through various theories.

My research has now placed Sir Francis Bacon in direct contact with the man who first received a charter for Nova Scotia. I'll expand on this connection in the following chapter, and although it is not a necessary part of my Oak Island theory, it is still very interesting.

What we generally know about the exploration of Nova Scotia is that Canada itself is said to have been explored, and perhaps even discovered by Sebastian Cabot, in 1497.

A French settlement was attempted in 1541, by Jacques Cartier. Some say this settlement was formed at Cape Sable Island, NS, others say at St. Croix, NS, and still others say it was along the St. Lawrence River, nearer to Quebec. Perhaps he tried several settlements.

On June 26, 1604, about 100 men sailed five French ships into the bay at the mouth of the St. Croix River that divides what is now New Brunswick and Maine, and established, on a small island which they named Île Ste.-Croix, the beginnings of a permanent French settlement in North America.

From Île Ste.-Croix the colonists would go on to found settlements in Nova Scotia and Quebec, building a lasting French presence on the continent.

Among those who arrived in 1604 was cartographer Samuel de Champlain. The leader of the fledgling colony was Pierre de Monts, who had been granted royal patents to exploit the fur trade in North America, and to establish the colony of Acadia.

While Champlain explored the Bay of Fundy and the coastline south to Maine, de Monts and his men cleared land and built dwellings on Île Ste.-Croix. However, rough living conditions forced them out and, in the summer of 1605, de Monts and Champlain dismantled the Île Ste.-Croix settlement and moved the colony across the Bay of Fundy to Port Royal, Nova Scotia.

In 1846, a stone was found near the old French fort remains at Port Royal, which had the date 1606 chiseled on it, along with other enigmatic symbols.

In 1613, on the grounds of an alleged encroachment on the English limits of Virginia, Captain Samuel Argall seized the French fort at Port Royal and dislodged the French settlers there, although many of them simply melted into the countryside as farmers and settlers. The French government filed no complaint at the time.

In 1620, the Plymouth Colony, famous for the U.S. Thanksgiving holiday, the ship *Mayflower*, and Plymouth Rock, was created in New England. The settlers of this colony, who were staunch Puritans, complained to the English king that there were French Catholics still living north of them, meaning the "dislodged" French settlers of Port Royal. On their behalf, Sir Frederick Gorges asked the king to take care of the matter. King James then consulted with Sir William Alexander on what could be done about this French problem.

In a paper published some time after this inquiry, Alexander refers to his first connection with the Nova Scotia scheme, writing: "Being much encouraged hereunto by Ferdinando (Frederick) Gorge and some utheris of the undertakers for New England, I shewed them that my countrymen would never adventure in such an enterprise, unless it were, as there was a New France, a New Spain, and a New England, that they might likewise have a New Scotland."

This was the very moment that the idea of settling Nova Scotia as a New Scotland was conceived.

It would be at Port Royal, in 1629, that William Alexander's son, William Jr., and the settlers provided for by the Baronets of Nova Scotia, would establish the first English colony, populated almost entirely by Scotsmen. The original group sent to New Scotland included seventy men (mostly skilled tradesmen) along with two women, presumably wives of two of these men. They spent the 1628-29 winter at Newfoundland, being kept from reaching Nova Scotia by bad weather.

My Oak Island theory involves the forced departure of these Scots from Port Royal in 1632, and their arrival on Oak Island, again due to bad weather.

Of course I wasn't aware of all this information when I first contacted the owners of Oak Island. I knew about the premier Baronet title, and other than a trip I had taken to Nova Scotia a decade ago, I really had no other specific knowledge about that land.

What I did have, however, was a burning curiosity about Oak Island, which began when I read a *Reader's Digest* article back in 1965. This same article has inspired many Oak Island enthusiast throughout the years.

What I also had, beyond curiosity, was a Fellowship with the Society of Antiquaries of Scotland, an honor I had earned after decades of researching and writing on Scottish history, along with three visits to Scotland.

And so, quite naturally, the folks at Oak Island began asking questions about how events in Scottish history could be related to events in Nova Scotia, especially concerning the Baronets of Nova Scotia. Soon, an hour-long telephone conversation took place between myself and an Oak Island historian. After sending along several informational e-mails, the next stage began when I was encouraged to write a book on the subject.

That book was *Oak Island Missing Links*, and in it I discussed many theories about Sir Henry Sinclair, the Mi'kmaq and *Zeno Narrative* legends, and the connection of the Knights Templar to families who also signed on to become Baronets of Nova Scotia.

I also provided information on the Templar presence in Scotland, and on several families who had links to both the Knights Templar and the Baronets of Nova Scotia, plus I identified two new items, which are invaluable Scottish artifacts that could have logically been taken to a New Scotland, and which have been missing from the old Scotland for a few centuries.

Once that book was published, I was invited to Oak Island to present my theories, at which point I expanded upon them considerably. Since that day, I have continued to send informational e-mails, and it was soon suggested that I write a follow-up book with my new information.

What I intend for this book to do is to focus, as much as possible, on the specific events that led up to and followed the year 1632 – the year, I believe, in which a ship sank in the so-called Oak Island swamp around the same time that additional items were buried in the Money Pit, and perhaps elsewhere on Oak Island.

As is true with the uncovering of most history, it has been an on-going and enjoyable effort to root out every bit of information I can find on this subject. And I believe I have a credible theory based on scientific data, including weather records, carbon dating of finished lumber found during Oak Island digs, plus depth soundings taken in the waters surrounding Oak Island, and including historical information found over several years of research, but most specifically in old documents related directly to my theory. This includes time spent exploring a private library at the Centre of Geographic Sciences (COGS), located in Lawrencetown, Nova Scotia.

At COGS, Doug Crowell, an ardent Oak Island historian himself, provided me with terrific new information gleaned from rare books, maps, and official reports. Though you may tend to only find what you are looking for, in every case during my visit, Doug's finds substantiated my broader theory to such a degree that I felt I had to work some of them, last minute, into my presentation set for the following day.

A lot was happening very quickly, but I could tell that new avenues of research had opened up, and so, when I returned to my home in Pennsylvania, I continued the effort to tell the story of Oak Island.

At some point, you have to cut off the research and report on the findings, and so that's what I have done with *Oak Island 1632*.

While I am as subject to making a mistake as anyone, I stand by my overall research and theories as being a credible explanation for the creation of a New Scotland in Nova Scotia, and the events leading up to the burial of items on Oak Island in the year 1632, along with the sinking of a ship in the swamp, which, at that time, could have been a cove open to the ocean.

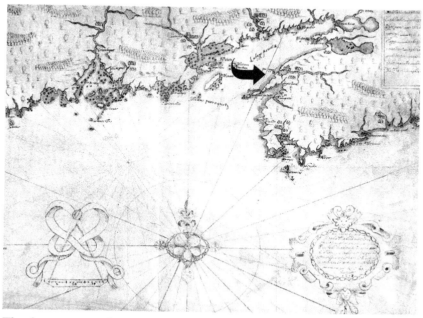

The above map was drawn by Samuel de Champlain at the French settlement of Port Royal, in 1607. While, unfortunately for us, it does not show Oak Island, it does actually show and name Port Royal, as indicated by the arrow.

Located in Victoria Park (Halifax, Nova Scotia), this cairn, built with stones from Sir William Alexander's Menstrie Castle, located in Scotland, concisely states his accomplishments:

Sir William Alexander
Writer, Statesman, Colonizer

His efforts to create a New Scotland
in the New World led to the
Royal Charter of Nova Scotia, 1621,

Attempts at settlement 1622-3,

The creating of the Order of
Knight Baronets of Nova Scotia 1624-5,

The Coat-of-Arms of Nova Scotia, 1626,

and the occupation of Port Royal
by Scottish settlers, 1629-32

Chapter Two
BACON AND ALEXANDER

The bulk of the story presented in this book takes place roughly in the first half of the 17th century. James Stuart was King of Scotland, as James VI, beginning in 1567, and King of England and Ireland, as James I, from March 1603, until his death on March 27, 1625.

James succeeded Queen Elizabeth I, who had been his own mother's executioner. With the combining of the kingdoms of Scotland, Ireland, and England, optimism, prosperity, and culture seemed to begin to work in synergy for James and his kingdom. Henry Hudson was setting off to find the Northwest Passage, New England was founded in the northeast corner of the American Colonies, and a New Scotland was to be founded in Nova Scotia through the efforts of Sir William Alexander.

Even Shakespeare's Globe Theater was drawing large, thoughtful crowds to witness his amazing, sophisticated dramas and comedies.

There has been much made over who might have actually authored some, if not all of Shakespeare's plays, and one of the main suspects has been Sir Francis Bacon. A persistent, but as yet unproven theory concerning Oak Island is that Bacon's manuscripts, including his original Shakespearean plays, are buried in the Money Pit.

The only circumstantial evidence so far has been vials of mercury found on Oak Island (once used to preserve buried documents), along with the recovery of a small piece of parchment paper just large enough to hold two handwritten letters, which was found in the Money Pit.

Of course, the authenticity and significance of these items, like many items found during Oak Island digs, could be questioned, and there is no proof either way.

We do know that Sir Francis Bacon had a link to Newfoundland through a land grant he received from James I, in 1610. We also now know that he had a link to Sir William Alexander, the first Baron of Nova Scotia.

Bacon had upset Queen Elizabeth, in 1593, when he criticized a tax she had levied, so when James I came along, Bacon was welcomed with open arms.

The following year (1594) Bacon published *Gesta Gragorum*. This was only the first of many books written by Bacon, on many subjects, most leaning towards the scientific point of view. What makes this book particularly interesting is that one of the stories in it refers to both the Knights Templar and a Shakespearean play.

The tales told in the book appear to have been reports of actual events. In one case, we learn: "The next grand night was intended to be upon Innocents' Day, at night; at which time there was a great presence of lords, ladies, and worshipful personages, that did expect some notable performance at that time; which, indeed, had been affected, if the multitude of beholders had not been so exceedingly great, that thereby there was no convenient room for those that were actors."

This event took place on December 28, 1594, at a place called Gray's Inn, located in London, England.

In the middle of the 12th century the Order of Knights Templar built a round church by the Thames River, which became known as the Temple Church. After the abolition of the Order in 1312, lawyers began to occupy the Temple site and its buildings. They formed themselves into two societies, the Inner Temple and Middle Temple, each of which was first mentioned by name in a manuscript yearbook dating to 1388.

The medieval Inns of Court, which included Lincoln's Inn and Gray's Inn, along with the Inner Temple and Middle Temple, were organized on the same basis as the colleges at Oxford and Cambridge Universities, offering accommodation to their students and facilities for education and dining.

The Inner Temple was paired up with Gray's Inn and the Middle Temple was paired up with Lincoln's Inn. This pairing of two sets of entities matches, to some degree, the theme of Shakespeare's play *The Comedy of Errors*, which involves two pairs of identical twins.

Bacon continues the story of this night at Gray's Inn by explaining that, "...our friend, the Inner Temple, determined to send their ambassador to our Prince of State, as lent from Frederick Templarius, their Emperor, who was then busied in his wars against the Turk. The Ambassador came very gallantly appointed, and attended by a great number of brave gentlemen, which arrived at our court about nine of the clock at night. Upon their coming thither, the King at Arms gave notice to the Prince, then sitting in his Chair of State in the Hall, that there was come to his court an ambassador from his ancient friend the State of Templaria, which desired to have present access unto his highness."

This Prince was actually Henry Helme, who was chosen as the "Christmas Prince" for this special gala event. The prince was visited by a Templar ambassador representing a Templar leader or "emperor," who was leading Knights Templar in battle against the Turks of the Holy Land. Whether this emperor was real or not is debatable. In the *Annals of Scotland* there is a description of the emperor of Liechtenstein requesting financial help from Elizabeth's successor, King James I, for money to help fight the Turks, and so this could have been a parody based on that type of request, or an actual visit by Templar type warriors still carrying on that battle.

A massive amount of confusion resulted when no actors could take the stage and so, as the story tells us: "The Lord Ambassador and his train thought that they were not so kindly entertained, as was before expected, and thereupon would not stay any longer at that time, but, in a sort, discontented and displeased. In regard whereof, as also for that the sports intended were especially for the gracing of the Templarians, it was thought good not to offer anything of account, saving dancing and revelling with gentlewomen; and after such sports, *The Comedy of Errors* was played by the Players. So that night was begun, and continued to the end, in nothing but confusion and errors; whereupon, it was ever afterwards called The Night of Errors."

This event marks the first-known performance of Shakespeare's *The Comedy of Errors*, and it took place in a setting rife with references to the Knights Templar, and to the inheritors of the Temple Church. Though Bacon originally wrote it in 1594, *Gesta Gragorum* wasn't fully published until 1623, in the midst of the attempted settlement of Nova Scotia, and it was then that it was printed at a shop located within the Temple Cloisters, which are still part of the Oxford University complex.

The point of this tale is that, during the time of the effort to create a New Scotland in Nova Scotia, the legends of the Knights Templar were still very strong and still being celebrated. Also, some would point to the first presentation of *The Comedy of Errors* being mentioned in *Gesta Gragorum* as an indication that Bacon may have had more than just a passing interest, and perhaps even a hand in the works of William Shakespeare.

Bacon went on to publish many other books in his lifetime including his *New Atlantis*, which describes a utopia being established to the west. William Alexander, at nearly the same moment in history, was in fact trying to establish a utopia to the west, in Nova Scotia.

Alexander was also a poet and playwright, publishing his first work in 1603, a book of sonnets called *Aurora*. As with his fellow Privy Council member Sir Francis Bacon, Sir William Alexander continued to publish many writings throughout his life.

That these two men served together in the court of King James I, and were both engaged in authoring substantial books and writings, would seem to indicate that they must have been close associates, if not very close friends. It would arguably be impossible for them not to know each other well, and their shared interest in writing books, poems and plays, and in creating utopias, would seem to connect them even further.

My theory of Oak Island revolves around the historical attempt by Alexander to settle Nova Scotia with Scots, and it seems that Bacon could not be unaware of Alexander's venture, and could well have asked him to take some of Bacon's writings to the New World for posterity and safe-keeping. It is known that Bacon was concerned with plagiarism and censorship, and it is reported that he had considered burying his manuscripts, and had discussed using mercury as a preservative.

Sir Francis, about this time, suffered a defeat by his political enemies and had actually been imprisoned for a short while during the same year that King James I granted Nova Scotia to William Alexander. It was King James who secured Bacon's released from prison.

Bacon was arrested in 1621. Alexander received his charter for Nova Scotia in 1621. Alexander sent ships to explore Nova Scotia in 1622 and 1623, and he formed the Baronets of Nova Scotia in 1625. Bacon wrote his utopia book, *New Atlantis,* from 1624 through 1626, though it wasn't published until 1627. Bacon died in 1626 and the first ships full of settlers left for Nova Scotia in 1628, finally settling there in 1629. It is easy to see that, historically speaking, these important events in each of these men's lives were essentially concurrent. This actually held true for other significant events in their lives, as well.

When the royal court of James VI of Scotland moved to London, in 1603, on James' accession to the English crown as James I, William Alexander moved with it, becoming Gentleman of the Privy Chamber and Master of the Household. In that same year, Sir Francis Bacon was knighted by James I. Sir William Alexander was knighted six years later, in 1609.

In 1604, Bacon was appointed as the King's Council and, by 1613, was made Attorney General of Great Britain. During this period William Alexander helped James I with the translation of the Psalms of King David, which was later separately published as *The Psalms of King David, translated by King James*, in 1631.

Alexander was appointed Master of Requests in 1614. His duties would have included the receiving of petitions from subjects, and presenting them for consideration by the Privy Council. The following year (1615), he was appointed to the Privy Council, and was followed by Sir Francis Bacon's appointment to the same body, in 1616.

In 1618, Bacon was appointed Lord Chancellor.

In 1626, the year Bacon died, James I appointed William Alexander to the post of Secretary of State.

With so many shared political contacts and positions, a jointly-held fascination with authorship, and Bacon's concern over his enemies destroying, censoring or plagiarizing his writings, it is not out of the question that Sir Francis could have asked Sir William to take some of his books and ideas to the New World, specifically to Nova Scotia, and that, due to a hurried exit from that land by the Scots, Bacon's works ended up on Oak Island.

Shown above is an engraving from the year 1900 showing the so-called **Domesday (Doomsday) Book**, also known as **The Great Survey**. The **Great Domesday** (the larger volume) and **Little Domesday** (the smaller volume), are shown in their 1869 bindings, lying on their older "Tudor-era" bindings. Several scholars credit this 11th century survey of a large portion of the British Isles with forcing many families to chose a specific surname, and many of these surnames remain intact from 1085 A.D. until today.

Chapter Three
DOOMSDAY

In my previous book, I wrote at length about the Knights Templar, often using information I personally received from a few of the highest level Templar historians in Scotland. Many of the people reading this book will have already heard of this mysterious group of religious warriors turned international bankers.

My opinion about a Templar connection to Nova Scotia (and thereby Oak Island) is not based on a belief that a group of these men actually visited there, dressed in their Templar garb and carrying a flag with a red cross on a white field. Instead, I feel that there was an indirect connection, which took place when families, once associated with the Knights Templar, accompanied explorers to this region, perhaps even bringing with them Templar treasures passed down through the ages.

It may be that descendents from later generations of clans, once connected to Templars, did accompany Sir Henry Sinclair, in 1398. But I am focusing specifically on the Scots settlement of Nova Scotia from 1629 through 1632. Even in this group of adventurers there were men who absolutely were members of clans that once had an association with the Knights Templar. And so I would next like to explore this part of my broader theory.

As I was presenting my information to the folks at Oak Island, one of the more specific requests from Rick Lagina was that I further explain the Knights Templar connection to the Baronets of Nova Scotia.

When I returned home, I almost immediately began looking at every single man on the list of Baronets to find any link of their family name to Templar lore. What I found is that about 25% of the surnames on the Baronets of Nova Scotia list also had a Knights Templar tradition somehow associated with their family name.

This was a somewhat amazing find in that many of the surnames on the list were not even created yet at the time of the Knights Templar.

Surnames in the British Isles came about in random fashion over many centuries. Many harken back to the *Domesday Book*, a survey of much of the British Isles, commissioned by William the Conqueror, in 1085 A.D.

As his conquered kingdom became better organized, William's goal was to collect taxes and any other wealth that might be due him, and so he insisted that families living in England and Wales identify themselves with a common surname that could be easily recognized.

Another book, the *Anglo-Saxon Chronicle*, makes reference to the *Domesday Book*, and its reason for existence. The *Anglo-Saxon Chronicle* states:

Then, at the midwinter [1085], was the king in Gloucester with his council ... After this had the king a large meeting, and very deep consultation with his council, about this land; how it was occupied, and by what sort of men. Then sent he his men over all England into each shire; commissioning them to find out how many hundreds of hides were in the shire, what land the king himself had, and what stock upon the land; or, what dues he ought to have by the year from the shire.

In order to record the above information the new king commanded the common folk and nobility alike to adopt a specific surname.

Perhaps entirely coincidental, Sir William Alexander's last substantial book of poems was also called *Doomes-Day*. He wrote the book in 1614, just on the verge of entering the most influential period of his life as Privy Council member and Baron of all of Nova Scotia.

The original *Domesday Book* manuscript still exists, and is usually held at The National Archives in London, England, but is sometimes loaned out. Many of the surnames in this book were chosen based on the location where the main family was living, or where they had come from – quite often back in Normandy.

For instance, one of the most famous Scottish names of all time is Bruce, as in King Robert the Bruce. The earlier version of the name was de Bruce, and the Bruce name came from Normandy, as well, very likely from the town of Briouze – thus the name de Briouze.

A name of significant importance to Oak Island theorists is that of de Sudeley. Based on the above theory, this name should represent someone who came from an area called Sudeley, and in fact, it does.

Sudeley is located just outside of Gloucester, where William the Conqueror issued his command that specific surnames should be adopted. The name originated with "leah" (a farm or enclosure) being added to "sud" (or south) denoting a farm south of the main village.

At first, there was simply a sacred well located at Sudeley said to have healing properties. Many pilgrims came there for healing. Then a chapel was built. Later a manor house was built, and finally Sudeley Castle.

When William demanded that surnames were to be taken, John, thought by some to be the son of King Harold (the very man William the Conqueror had conquered) was living at Sudleah, or, as it was given in the *Domesday Book*, "Sudledge."

John took the surname de Sutlie, which eventually became de Sudeley.

John's son was Ralph de Sudeley, a great benefactor of religious orders, who also gave the Knights Templar several major plots of land.

In the poem "The legend of Ralph de Sudeley," written in the 19th century, it states: *"It was good Ralph de Sudeley come back from the Paynim wars, and he bore the title of his fame scored in a hundred scars."*

At the time, the Turks were also called the Paynims.

It appears from the poem that Ralph was killed by a Paynim. He was very vocal: *"De Sudeley, when in foreign lands, had often heard recount, what deeds of ill the Assassins did, those murderers of the Mount. And ever anon he raised his voice in bitter mirth, and swore he'd count it Christian sport to hunt them (the Paynim) from the earth."*

Ralph kept a hound at his gate as a watchdog. One evening he and his chaplain heard the dog barking.

The women and children were ushered away, apparently after some type of intrusion, and according to the poem, *"Twas a human form, and the chaplain prayed that the soul (of de Sudeley) had gotten grace, and the Baron shook as the high-held torch flashed on de Sudeley's face. A dagger's point was in his back, and graven on its blade, 'Hoc propter versa tua,' – This, 'For words which thou hast said.'"*

In other words de Sudeley had been assassinated by the Paynims for all the angry words he had said about them.

What is of special interest to us is that de Sudeley is said to have brought artifacts back from the Holy Land, with some speculating that the Ark of the Covenant was among them, and perhaps a piece of the cross of Jesus, or other sacred objects.

Others have speculated that he was a Templar himself, which would make sense since he fought in the Crusades, and was a benefactor of the Templars.

There is said to be a record that he had "objets sacrés" at Sudeley Castle and charged pilgrims to see them.

One theory says that, while serving as commander of a small garrison of Templars at the ruins of the ancient city of Petra, in 1188 A.D., de Sudeley found the hidden Ark of the Covenant, and brought it back with him to Castle Sudeley, in England.

Queen Elizabeth visited Sudeley Castle three times. The final time was when England was under threat from the Spanish Armada, in 1588. Of course this was just a few short years before her nephew James VI of Scotland took her place as James I of England (1603), and it was directly during the time that Sir William Alexander was establishing himself as a major player, first in Scotland and then in England. James I and Sir William were the driving force behind the Baronets of Nova Scotia.

Charles I, son of James I, attacked Sudeley Castle during the civil war that saw him finally lose his head to Oliver Cromwell, whose men had taken over the castle. Cromwell also plays a role in this story.

But there is an entirely new and exciting connection to be made here through the Baronets of Nova Scotia.

The de Sudeley family seems to disappear from England in the mid-1300s, with one line ending in Spain, upon the death of a later John de Sudeley. The title of Baron of Sudeley fell into abeyance when this third Baron died, in 1367. It was later regenerated, but by a man named Boteler, not someone named de Sudeley.

At nearly the exact same time, the de Suttie family appears in Scotland, in an area called Balgone, or more recently called Balgonie. The de Suttie name means the same thing as de Sudeley – "a farm to the south, or in the south." It is also recorded as de Suddie and de Suddy.

In England, the de Sudeleys no longer owned Sudeley Castle. King Edward VI, of England, granted Sudeley Castle to his uncle, Thomas Seymour. Later, it came into the hands of the Brydges family, and they owned it when Queen Elizabeth visited the castle.

Meanwhile, the de Suttie or de Suddie family grows in Scotland, eventually dropping the "de" prefix, and here is the important link – Number 107 of the Baronets of Nova Scotia is, in fact, Sir George Suttie of Balgone!

Q. What else happened in the early to mid-1300s?

A. The Knights Templar were dissolved!

Many spelling variations for both the de Sudeley name and the de Suttie name are recorded, and they both mean the exact same thing – "a farm to the south."

What stands out is that the original name taken at the time of the *Domesday Book* was spelled de Sutlie, and the main Scottish spelling was de Suttie. Note, there is only one letter difference between these two spellings.

One name disappears from England in roughly the same generation as the other one appears in Scotland.

Knights Templar are hunted everywhere, at this same point in history, except for in Scotland.

It seems more than just likely that the de Sudeley family, due to the family's involvement with the Knights Templar, and the loss of Sudeley Castle, took refuge in Scotland, and also very likely took their Holy Land relics with them. As with many names in Scottish history, the de Sudeley name may have taken on another form (one of many) as de Suttie, and, Sir George Suttie of Balgone later becomes a Baronet of Nova Scotia.

It is entirely possible that relics once secreted away at Sudeley Castle were among the items spirited out of Scotland, hidden in the ships of Sir William Jr., which had been given a "safe passage" letter by King Charles.

I tell more in the following chapter about these ships that left for Nova Scotia in 1628, carrying a letter of safe passage from the king.

In the Gaelic Highlands of Scotland, surnames were not affected much by the *Domesday Book* instructions to create specific surnames. There, a man was often recorded with a given name followed by his descent from several men, generally as far back as the clan bard could reasonably feel safe in repeating.

An example of this is to be found not in Scotland but in Nova Scotia, in the book *Tales Until Dawn: The World of a Cape Breton Gaelic Story-Teller*. Here, a man is recorded as "Murchadh Mac'Illemhaoil (Murchadh Dhómhnaill 'ic Nill 'ic Iain 'ic Mhurchaidh 'ic Dhómhnaill)."

We would understand this man to be named Murdoch MacDonald, son of Neil, son of John, son of Murdoch, son of Donald. This is only one of many examples that could be given of the recording of Gaelic surnames in this manner.

Finally, we have names that come from occupations. These are sometimes referred to as by-names or T-names. Examples would be Miller, Smith, Fisher, Arrowsmith, Butcher, Abbot, Carpenter, Butler... the list goes on.

It can easily be seen how sticky it could get in trying to connect surnames from the time of the Knights Templar to the time of the Baronets of Nova Scotia. And yet I made this attempt in a report I sent off to the folks at Oak Island to show just how dramatically linked the Knights Templar were to the Baronets of Nova Scotia.

Each list of Baronets of Nova Scotia varies, depending on when it was compiled. For my report I used a list of the shields portraying the Arms of Baronets of Nova Scotia, which is on display in the Commemoration Room at

Menstrie Castle, home to Sir William Alexander, as this would appear to be the most official list available.

It is impossible to link all the names since many of them originated after the time of the Knights Templar.

In addition to the de Sudeley name, what I have done in this report is to identify as many Baronet surnames as I can reasonably find that also have a connection to Templar traditions or land transfers. This may not be a complete list, but it is definitely an impressive one.

Two names that don't appear on the Menstrie Castle list are Sir William Alexander, who began the Baronets program, and Sir Robert Gordon, to whom Alexander gave all of Cape Breton.

It is also worth noting that William Alexander Jr., the man who led the Scots settlers in Nova Scotia, and his brother Anthony, joined the Freemasons just two years after returning to Scotland. They were the world's first two Freemasons, thus further connecting the Knights Templar, the Baronets of Nova Scotia, and the Freemasons in one nearly continuous history. More on this to come.

Following Sir William Alexander and Sir Robert Gordon, I will list each Baronet/Templar surname using its position on the list of Baronets. In some cases, the same surname is listed in more than one position, so that two or more numbers will introduce that surname.

Sir William Alexander had a connection to the Knights Templar through the MacDonald Clan, having descended directly from Alexander MacDonald, the uncle of the man who, it is said, led Templars at the Battle of Bannockburn – one Angus Og MacDonald.

There were many Templar holdings and Templar graves scattered throughout Clan Donald territory. In addition, the Chiefs of Clan Donald were supporters of Paisley Abbey for centuries. The first owner of the abbey was one of the original financial supporters of the Knights Templar. See the entry for numbers 14, 15, 26, 27, and 64, on the following pages, for more on this man.

William Alexander's family received former Templar lands. On file in the Scottish Public Record Office, in Edinburgh, Scotland, there is reference to the Alexanders inheriting Templar lands at Menstrie, in 1537, and again in 1553. Menstrie Castle is, in fact, built on former Knights Templar land. Can you get any closer of a connection?

Sir Robert Gordon's family also has some interesting Templar traditions. To begin with, in 1270, Sir Robert's ancestor Adam de Gordon took part in the Crusade organized by Louis XI, of France. From this fact the family is said to derive their crest and motto.

Also, in 1309, Sir Adam de Gordon, in return for giving up certain temporal claims, obtained from the monks of Kelso permission to possess a private chapel nearby. The Abbey of Kelso is associated with the Knights Templar concerning a dispute over the building of a nearby chapel thought to have been the one involving Sir Adam Gordon, an apparent Knights Templar himself.

It was this same Sir Adam de Gordon who was sent to Rome by King Robert the Bruce, in 1320, as the bearer of the famous Declaration of Arbroath, or Scottish declaration of independence. Many of the surnames I am speaking of here, as appearing on the Knights Templar list, and on the Baronets of Nova Scotia list, also appear as signatures on the Declaration of Arbroath.

The seat of the Gordon family is even today located at Aboyne Castle, also once owned by the Knights Templar. (Two additional Gordon men are on the Baronets list.)

While the remaining names I mention don't include all of those on the Menstrie Castle Baronets of Nova Scotia list, they represent a large percentage of them. They are listed in the order that their title was created.

Nos. 1 & 20 – The Innes of Innes Baronetcy, from the city of Elgin, was created in Nova Scotia, on May 28, 1625, for Sir Robert Innes. He was the very first Baronet. The second Innes Baronetcy of Nova Scotia was created on January 15, 1628, for another Robert Innes, of Balvenie, being No. 20. This line failed on the death of the 8th Baronet of this line, in 1817. Finally, a third Innes Baronetcy was created on March 20, 1686, for Alexander Innes, of Coxton, a member of the Scottish Parliament for the County of Moray, Scotland, though he is not shown on the Menstrie Castle list.

The Innes clan descends, in part, from Sir Henry Sinclair's daughter, Elizabeth, and her husband, John Drummond. The first barony is from the very seat of Innes, which was originally a piece of land located between two rivers in the County of Moray.

One of the many things that the County of Moray (previously known as Nairn) is noted for is its association with the Knights Templar.

During the very same centuries that the Innes clan controlled the Innes lands in Moray, parts of the countryside in and about nearby Ardersier (also located in County Moray) were owned by the Order of the Knights Templar. These lands were referred to as "Temple Land," "Temple Cruik," and "Temple Bank."

The distance between the ancient seat of the Innes House and Ardersier is less than an hour's drive by automobile, today.

The *History of the Province of Moray*, a book from 1886, when speaking of the Templars, states, "They had some lands in Ardersier... The Templars had a house in the town of Elgin (also the seat of Clan Innes); and, at Kinermony, in Aberlour..." Kinermony is located only about twelve miles from Elgin.

Ardersier, Elgin and Kinermony have traditions, and some official records, showing a Templar presence, and all lie within an hour's drive of the seat of the Innes clan. Add to this their family's relationship to Sir Henry Sinclair, and the Innes surname being attached to the Baronets of Nova Scotia list becomes very significant.

Nos. 2, 18 & 28 – Four Campbell men are listed on the Menstrie Castle Baronets list, Sir Duncan Campbell being listed as the second Baronet.

Colin Campbell is No. 18. Dugald Campbell is No. 28. A fourth Campbell, Donald, does not appear on the Menstrie list, although he still held a Baronet title.

An earlier Colin Campbell supported Bruce at Bannockburn and may have been a Knights Templar. The Campbell family has a tradition that one Colin Campbell was a valiant warrior considered a Templar by the Campbell family. He spent time away from home in Europe and in Palestine, during the later Crusades. Apparently, because of the persecution of the Templars, Sir Colin had to make the trip home from Rome disguised as a beggar. Campbell family tradition says that he returned just in time to prevent his wife, who thought he had been killed, from marrying another man. To his wife's surprise, he "shrugged off his rags to reveal the white cloak and scarlet cross of the Knights Templar."

The authors of *The Temple And The Lodge* suggest that Templars fought under the guise and colors of Clan Campbell at Bannockburn, greatly aiding the Scots victory. If this is true, it would explain Clan Campbell's sudden growth in numbers and strength, as well as their expectation of property and titles from the king, in reward for their service.

No. 3 – The third Baronet was Donald MacDonald who descended from Angus Og MacDonald, who, many sources say led Knights Templar at Bannockburn.

Nos. 4 & 86 – Sir John Colquhoun (Calhoun) of Luss (located on the shores of Loch Lomond) was the fourth Baronet of Nova Scotia. The Colquhouns were originally the Kilpatricks or Kirkpatricks of Ireland. Kilpatrick would originate with Gillepatrick or "servant of St. Patrick." Kirkpatrick would mean "church of St. Patrick." Kirkpatrick of Closeburn is listed as No. 86 on the Menstrie list. This would have been essentially the same extended family as the Colquhouns.

At the Old Kilpatrick Church in Dumbartonshire, the same shire where Luss is located, there is what appears, by all indications, to be a Templar gravestone.

It is less than 17 miles from this Templar gravestone to the home of one of the Baronets of Nova Scotia.

"Humphry Colquhoun, Knight," rendered homage to the Scottish king in 1296. He later witnessed a charter issued by Robert the Bruce to Sir John Colquhoun in 1308. He received a charter for the barony of Luss from Bruce, also in 1308, for "special services, and for never having deserted the king's interest."

At the very least, Humphry Colquhoun was a Knight serving under Robert the Bruce. It may be that it is his grave located near the Colquhoun town of Luss that shows a connection to the Knights Templar.

No. 5 – Sir John Leslie was the fifth registered Baronet. The Leslie family has a large number of connections through marriage, and otherwise, to the MacDonalds, Sinclairs, Stewarts and others – too extensive to go into, in this report. However, one of their main Templar connections is that, on January 23, 1623, they are officially recorded as holding (amongst many other properties), "the Templar lands of Kothmurriell or Christskirk," and of "Temple Croft" – again, a very close connection!

No. 6 – Sir William Graham is sixth on the list. The Graham family owns the Church of Arthuret, located in Longtown, England. Legend has it that this is where many Knights Templar escaped to, from France. The church displays Templar, Masonic and Holy Grail symbology, much like the Sinclair Rosslyn Chapel.

Nos. 7 & 30 – Sir William Forbes of Monymusk became Baronet No. 7. Sir William Forbes of Craigievar is listed as No. 30. Monymusk and Craigievar are located near Aberdeen, Scotland. Having lived in the area for many generations, the Forbes family, in 1436, purchased the land known as Fiddes, near Aberdeen. The nearby Temple of Fiddes was on lands formerly owned by, and associated with the Knights Templar, who, while in their heyday, were based at Maryculter (southwest of Aberdeen), and had quite extensive lands in this area.

Nos. 8 & 104 – Sir George Johnstone of Caskieben is eighth on the list. A Johnstone of Westerhall is also listed as No. 104 on the Menstrie list. Sir George was actually born at Forbes Castle in Aberdeen and married into the Forbes family, so he would share, to some degree, any relationship the Forbes family had with the Templars. The later Johnstone almost certainly descended from George Johnstone, and from the Forbes family.

No. 9 – Thomas Burnett became the ninth Baronet of Nova Scotia in 1626. The earliest known Burnett was Robert Burnett from 1128. Later, Sir Alexander Burnett, Knight, traveled with Robert the Bruce, as he hid from the English before Bannockburn. It is not known if he was a Knights Templar or simply a Scottish Knight, but since Bruce is thought to have been a Templar, there is the possibility that Burnett was also a Templar.

Nos. 14, 15, 26, 27, 64 – Bruce and Stewart/Stuart. These names are forever linked in Scottish history as Robert the Bruce's grandson became the first Stewart King of Scotland when Bruce's daughter married the "Steward" of Scotland. There was one Bruce Baronet (No. 26, Sir William Bruce), one Stuart Baronet (No. 14, Sir James Stuart), and three Stewart Baronets.

The Stewarts included No. 15, Sir James Stewart, No. 27, Sir Arthur Stewart, and No. 64, Stewart of Greenock, plus two additional Stewart Baronets that don't appear on the Menstrie Castle list.

Robert the Bruce is thought to have been a Templar himself, and was aided at the Battle of Bannockburn by fellow Knights Templar according to some traditions.

In 1189, Alan FitzWalter, the 2nd Lord High Steward of Scotland was a benefactor of the Order of Knights Templar. It is from his family that Robert II, grandson of Robert the Bruce, and the first Stewart King of Scotland, also descends. The 1189 record is one of the most direct links of the Templars to the Baronets of Nova Scotia.

Also descending from Robert the Bruce and the Steward of Scotland were James I and Charles I of England, the men who chartered the Baronets of Nova Scotia. How much closer of a connection can be found?

Nos. 23, 24 & 73 – The name Murray appears three times on the Menstrie list, No. 23 being Sir Archibald Murray, No. 24 being Sir Patrick Murray, and No. 73 being Murray of Ochtertyre. Three additional Murray men were Baronets but do not appear on the Menstrie list, these being two Williams and a Richard Murray.

The Murray name is a form of Moray, from County Moray. We've already seen, from the Innes listing, how prominent the Knights Templar were in County Moray.

A house in County Moray, known as Temple House, was once owned by Patrick Murray, Baronet of Nova Scotia. Sir Robert Moray, son and grandson of a Baronet, was one of the earliest, most famous Freemasons.

Nos. 35, 44 & 113 – Sir James Sinclair is listed as No. 35 on the Baronets list. Another James Sinclair is listed as No. 44. Sinclair of Dunbeath is listed as No. 113.

The Sinclair family has a rich history of connection to the Knights Templar, which doesn't need to be repeated here. However, the interests of these three Sinclair men, and the three Innes men who all signed up as Baronets of Nova Scotia (and who all likely descended from Henry Sinclair) certainly helps link his voyage to the later attempt by the Baronets to settle Nova Scotia.

No. 37 – Sir Lachlan MacLean is the 37th listed Baronet of Nova Scotia. An earlier "Sir Lachlan MacLean-de Corzon, Baron of ak'ham," fought in the Third Crusade as a Templar. The suffix "de Corzon", or "of Corzon," has been used as a metaphor for the Sacred Heart of Jesus. The addition of Baron of ak'ham is likely a reference to this Lachlan being part of the Templars that were known to be stationed in the Israeli city of Acre, which, in Hebrew, is often spelled Akko, and in Arabic, is often written as Akkā, meaning "wise man." This shows a direct connections of a Baronet of Nova Scotia family to the Knights Templar.

The MacLean saga continues. James Hector MacLean was the second Grand Master of the French Freemasons, in the early 1700s. James was still Chief of Clan Maclean, at Duart Castle, Isle of Mull, Scotland, when he was promoted to Grand Master of this French organization that he had helped to get started. It was on the Isle of Mull where some Templars are thought to have landed when escaping to Scotland from France.

But there's more to the MacLean story. John Smith was one of the first three young treasure hunters on Oak Island, and also one of the earliest owners of the lot that included the Money Pit. His mother was a MacLean.

Therefore, in the MacLean family, alone, we have: a recorded Knights Templar; the 37th Baronet of Nova Scotia; a very significant Masonic leader; and one of the earliest owners and treasure hunters of the Money Pit!

No. 43 – Alexander Abercrombie (and "Sandilands of Sandilands.") In 1637, Alexander Abercrombie was created a Baronet of Nova Scotia. In 1628, the Chief of the Sandilands Clan was also made a Baronet, though he is not on the Menstrie Castle list. The land of Abercrombie dates back to the earliest history of Scotland and was, at one point, the home to the Sandilands family, who, it is thought, became the "Sandilands of Abercrombie," and who eventually adopted just the Abercrombie surname.

James Sandilands, Lord Abercrombie, received a charter from Mary, Queen of Scots, for the possession of three Knights Templar and Knights of St. John properties in Scotland, on January 24, 1563. It has been claimed that, in Scotland, the Templar Order combined with the Hospitallers and continued as The Order of St John and the Temple until the Reformation. When Sir James Sandilands, Preceptor of the Order, converted to Protestantism in 1553, the Order of St John and the Temple is said to have ceased to exist.

One of the names not on the Menstrie Castle list, but generally accepted as a Baronet of Nova Scotia, is that of "Cadell of Cadell" or the Chief of Clan Cadell. According to *The Surnames of Scotland,* by George Black, the name Cadell was used to disguise members of the Calder family. It is interesting to note that the first name of the Cadell chief is not given, nor does their surname appear on the Menstrie list. William Cadell served as a Knights Templar from October 1212 to May 1213, and again from March 1229 to June 1232. He is also listed as "Guillaume Cadeil, Master of England," in 1214. This is another one of the most direct links of Baronet of Nova Scotia surnames to Knights Templar surnames.

Another name not listed but generally accepted as belonging on the Baronets list is that of Sir Edward Moir. The Moir name is interchangeable with the de la More name, in Scotland. Guillaume de la More served as a Templar from 1298–1307, the year of suppression of the Order. When he refused to confess, de la More, the last English Master of The Temple, was placed in the Tower of London, where he eventually died.

Approximately one-quarter of the surnames on the Menstrie Castle list of Baronets of Nova Scotia, along with a handful of other Baronet names not listed there, have been very closely connected, in one way or another, to the Knights Templar. To go beyond this effort would belabor the point, although there are very likely Knights Templar connections with many additional surnames on the Menstrie Castle list, or for that matter on other versions of the Baronets of Nova Scotia list.

Additional names on the Baronets list are absolutely connected through marriage or alliances with surnames included in this analysis, and share their histories.

It is obvious that many illustrious families of Scotland played a role in both the history of the Knights Templar in Scotland and, later, in the attempt of the Baronets of Nova Scotia to plant settlers in Nova Scotia, even to eventually include ownership of the Money Pit lot by a MacLean descendant! Baronet titles continued to be granted until 1706, and the last settlement involving a Baronet land case in Nova Scotia took place in 1733.

While the Scots were ousted from Nova Scotia in 1632, and the selling of actual land tracts ended in 1638, efforts to remain involved in Nova Scotia may not have ended so abruptly, an idea I will discuss later.

While more connections could possibly be found, there can be no question in the reader's mind that the Baronet of Nova Scotia families had very substantial connections to Knight Templar traditions and lands. This doesn't prove that Templar treasure was taken to Nova Scotia by Baronet settlers, but it at least allows for that possibility in a way not previously proposed.

As we know, Templar wealth had to go somewhere. That some of it transferred into the hands of Templar related families has already been proven, beyond doubt, through the transfer of many land grants of former Knights Templar properties into the hands of Baronet of Nova Scotia families. Other Knights Templar wealth and artifacts could have quietly and logically followed a similar path. And that path could have led to their transference to Nova Scotia on ships that could not be inspected or stopped due to a "safe passage" letter from the king, himself. That story is next!

Chapter Four
SAFE PASSAGE

So, let's say, just for the sake of argument, that we've established enough of a connection between the families, whose leaders signed on to become Baronets of Nova Scotia, and traditions and/or land grants related to the Knights Templar, to assume that, through these families, some of these treasures might have been taken to Nova Scotia, and, through happenstance, have ended up on Oak Island. And let's assume that perhaps even some of Francis Bacon's manuscripts could have followed suit.

Even if Templar treasures or artifacts were passed down to later generations within these clans, how could they be taken to Nova Scotia unnoticed? How could Bacon's works, or other missing, but important Scottish artifacts (which I will identify later as possible items taken to Nova Scotia) also travel there unnoticed?

Luckily, we have the answer!

King Charles I is the man who chartered the Baronets of Nova Scotia. He was the son of James I, the man who gave Nova Scotia to Sir William Alexander.

On March 26, 1628, Charles wrote, from the Palace of Whitehall, a letter of safe passage for "Sir William Alexander, Younger," or, as we would say, "William Alexander Junior."

The letter states very specifically that no one was to bother William Jr., or inspect or delay his four ships as they left for Nova Scotia. I am repeating the actual words from this safe passage letter to show how extreme and specific the word of Charles I were:

*Whereas the four schippis belonging to Sir William Alexander knight, sone to Sir William Alexander, our Secretarie for Scotland: whareof they are to be set out towards Newfoundland, the River of Canada, and New Scotland for the settling of Colonies in those partes, and for other thare laufull affaires: Theis are, tharefore, to will and require you, and every one of you, to permitt and suffer the said schippes, and every one of them, with thare wholl furnature, goods, merchandice, schips companies, and planters, queitlie and peaceabbillie in thare going thither, returning from thence, or during thare being further in any other parts whatsoever, till they shall happin to returne to any of our dominiones, **to pass by you, without any of your lettes (hinderances)**, stayes, troubles, imprestis of ther men, or any others men, or any other hinderance whatsoever: whareof you shall not faill.*

In other words, "Leave these four ships alone!"

We are so lucky to have a transcript of this letter because, in 1827, a book was published which contained transcripts of all the official information that could be found concerning the Nova Scotia settlement. This book was identified with the long title *Royal Letters, Charters, and Tracts Relating To The Colonization Of New Scotland And The Institution Of The Order Of The Knights Baronets Of Nova Scotia 1621 – 1638.*

The safe passage letter was only part of all that was transcribed. There was so much more. For one thing, we know for sure the names of at least two of the ships mentioned, and their cargo capacity. This cargo capacity is important if we are looking at whether these Scottish settlers had enough room to transport significant items to Nova Scotia unnoticed, due to the safe passage letter.

The first ship we hear of through this book is the *Eagle*, which has a burthen or cargo capacity of one-hundred and twenty tons. In the United States, a ton equals 2,000 pounds, but in England, a ton equals 2240 pounds. This means that the *Eagle* had a carrying capacity of 268,800 pounds.

The second ship, the *Morning Star*, was even larger. Its burthen was 300 tons, or 672,000 pounds of potential cargo capacity.

This means the *Eagle* and the *Morning Star* had a combined ability to carry 940,800 pounds of cargo, not including the ship's crew or their belongings – nearly one million pounds of something.

I have just recently found information on the other two ships not listed by name in this book. It seems safe to assume that they would have the capacity to carry at least another half-million pounds of cargo.

Keep in mind that, in 1628, most items, except for things like weapons and tools, were made from organic, and thus lighter weight substances. So you could pack an awful lot into a million-and-a-half pounds of storage area. And all of these items, due to King Charles' letter, were exempt from any interference or inspection.

Just a week before the safe passage letter was written by King Charles I, he issued another proclamation naming William Alexander Sr. as Admiral of Nova Scotia. Dated March 18, 1628, the document reads:

Forsameekle ("seeing as how," or "considering that") as the Kings Majesty by his letters patent under the Great Seale hes mad and constitute Sir William Alexander knight Admirall of New Scotland; for the better exercicing of which office necessar it is that there be a Seal of the Admiralty of said kingdom. Thairfore the Lords of Secreit Counsell ordanis and commands Charles Dickieson, sinkear of his Majesteis yrnes, to make grave and sinke ane Seale of the office of Admiralty of New Scotland, to be the proper Seale of the said office. The said Seale having a shippe with all her ornaments and apparralling, the mayne saile onlie displayed with the armes of New Scotland, and upon the head of the said shippe careing ane unicorn sittand and ane savage man standing upoun the sterne, both bearing St. Androes Croce (St. Andrew's Cross)..."

The Coat of Arms of Nova Scotia still carries the unicorn and the "savage" man.

Also, the Canadian Navy has in its service an ice breaker named the *CCGS Sir William Alexander*.

I have since discovered the names of the other two ships that sailed with the *Eagle* and the *Morning Star*. William Jr. led these four ships to Nova Scotia, along with Sir George Home, Baronet of Nova Scotia, serving as his assistant. The other two ships mentioned in the king's safe passage letter appear, based on privateer records, to be the *Alexander* and the *James*.

The *Alexander* was likely named for the Alexander family and the *James* for King James. These ships were both under the command of David Alexander.

David was a close cousin to William Alexander. As best I could trace his family line, it also originated at Menstrie Castle, as did William's. There is a government document signed by both William Alexander and David Alexander. Regardless of the exact relationship, these men obviously knew each other well, since it was David's privateering vessels that set off to accompany William's two passenger/cargo ships.

Entrepreneurs converted many different types of vessels into privateers, including obsolete warships and refitted merchant ships. The investors would arm the vessels and recruit large crews, much larger than a merchantman or a naval vessel would carry, in order to man the prizes they captured. So it is safe to assume that the *James* and the *Alexander* were large enough to hold another half-million pounds of cargo, if not more.

In fact, David Alexander received a warrant from Sir Archibald Napier for the "outrecking (outfitting) of the shippe callit the *Alexander* and sometime callit the *James*, whairof David Alexander and James Binning wer captans, and furnishing of the saids shippes with poulder, shott and other necessars, and for the wages, meit and drinke of the captanes and everie ane of the companie of the saids shippes..."

David is mentioned in *Memorials of the Earl of Stirling and of the House of Alexander, Volume 1*, written by Charles Rogers, in 1877. Here we read that, in letters of reprisal granted by Charles I under the Great Seal, on April 20, 1626, he is styled "Captain David Alexander, master of a ship of Anstruther called the *James.*"

By these letters, David was empowered "on account of injuries done to the King of England by the King of Spain, to arm and fit out his ship, and go to sea and pursue, attack, and sink all ships of Spain..." (*Registrum Magni Sigilli Regum Scotorum, or the Register of the Great Seal of Scotland, lib. ii. No 360, fol. 249*).

David is mentioned again on July 22, 1626, as "owner of the good ship called the *James...*" (*Register of Deeds, vol. 506*).

On April 2, 1627, the king wrote his exchequer asking him to carry on with the appointment of David Alexander as "Chieffe Work Maister for fortifications within our kingdome..." (*Register of Letters*).

The "Chieffe Work Maister" or Master of Works oversaw all major building construction within Scotland and was a much sought after and fought for position.

The Exchequer was a government position responsible for collecting revenue and making payments on behalf of the king, auditing official accounts, and trying legal cases relating to revenue.

Our story revolves, to a considerable degree, around the eventual appointment of Anthony Alexander, brother to William Alexander Jr. (who led the settlement attempt in Nova Scotia) to the same position of Master of Works for Scotland, not long after the above record was written. After Anthony's untimely death, even he was replaced by another Alexander, Anthony's brother Henry.

In fact, Anthony Alexander's appointment to the position of Master of Works is central to the story told in this book, and to the very formation of the Freemasons!

David served for awhile under the King of Poland as a mercenary, and, in Scotland, he continued to grow in political power and position, until August, 1651, when he was captured by the troops of Oliver Cromwell, who also plays a role in the story told within these pages.

In the book *Terror Of The Seas: Scottish Maritime Warfare 1513-1713*, written by Steve Murdoch, the author speaks of the *Eagle* and the *Morning Star*. He also tells us that David Alexander commanded the *James* and *Alexander*, and how the latter ship took a Portuguese ship, in 1629, and drove it into the port at Plymouth, England.

This author states that the *Alexander* took two French ships on her very first voyage in 1627. This would have been the year before the Scottish settlers, under the leadership of William Alexander Jr., set out for Port Royal, Nova Scotia.

There is a story that one of David's ships cut short its involvement in this trip to Nova Scotia. In one record, it is stated that the *James*, being captained by an associate of David (likely James Binning) spied an enemy ship that he wished to capture, and so he let his Scottish settlers off on the coast of Scotland and took off after the prize. I found two additional versions of this story, only in these cases, it is said that it was the *Alexander* that left the fleet. Whichever ship it was, the *James* or the *Alexander*, it appears that perhaps only three ships made the voyage to Nova Scotia under the younger William.

Steve Murdoch's *Terror Of The Seas* book was helped along by many knowledgeable scholars. It sells for around $200 on most online book stores, and is a book that can be counted on as an extremely sincere effort to catalog Scottish privateers and their undertakings.

One paragraph from this book stands out:

The Scots under Sir William's authority carried the war further than most privateers by actually conducting amphibious operations. Four vessels sailed for Nova Scotia in 1629 (actually it was 1628) with William Lord Alexander (William Jr.) and a second group with Robert Gordon of Lochinvar. A mixed British contingent, under the leadership of David Kirk, pushed right up the St. Lawrence River and captured Quebec, a prize not returned to the French until 1632, despite the Peace of Sousa in April 1629.

This return of Nova Scotia to France, along with its lead up and aftermath, is the very story I am telling with my *Oak Island 1632* book.

The *Eagle* was most likely William Alexander Jr.'s flagship. The *Morning Star*, having the largest cargo capacity, was likely the main cargo ship. And the *James* and the *Alexander* were meant to serve as protection, sailing alongside the other two ships, until one or the other left the fleet to pursue another prize.

We now have a fairly clear picture of the fleet that left the Isle of Man, in 1628, bound for Nova Scotia. In addition to the crews of each ship, there were 70 men and two women who were to settle near the old French fort of Port Royal, which became Annapolis Royal.

The *Morning Star* was docked at Dumbarton, Scotland, for quite awhile, as settlers were encouraged to make the voyage, and supplies were gathered. Meanwhile, the *Eagle* waited on the River Thames, in London, until its sister ship was ready. She sailed to Scotland to meet the *Morning Star*, and these two ships apparently met up with the *James* and the *Alexander* at the Isle of Man, from where they are said to have begun their journey west.

Though they left the British Isles in 1628, they did not make it to Nova Scotia until 1629, spending their first winter in Newfoundland. They were asked to leave Nova Scotia in 1632. That departure is central to my theory, as I will soon show.

Sir William Alexander, himself, was implicated in an act of privateering, at least indirectly, early in 1632, when he captured a German ship. It is likely, considering his age and high position in government, that this ship was actually captured by David Alexander, in the name of William. In the Privy Council records we read:

Complaint by Walter Reynick, master of the ship called the St. Lawrence of Lubick (part of Germany), as follows – His ship was upon her due course laden with salts, when she was violently seized by Sir William Alexander, knight, Master of Stirline, and the greater part of the crew set on shore in France, of whom the comlainer has since heard nothing. Sir William then brought the ship to Leith where within a short time she was adjuged a prize, but most unlawfully so because (1) the ship carried no prohibited goods from or to Spain, (2) the Admiral and his deputies never cited the complainer nor other persons interested in the ship to any trial, and (3) the said William, the better to obtain the end he desired, put away those persons from the ship who could have cleared her of this accusation."

How this matter was resolved is yet to be discovered, but it would not be surprising if Sir William won the day. His influence at the court of the king was nearly unmatched. He was able to get his son Anthony named to the covetous position of Master of Works for Scotland against the political pressure and power of William Sinclair, descendant of William Sinclair, builder of Rosslyn Chapel, and of Henry Sinclair, the man some say made a trip to Nova Scotia in 1398.

This later William Sinclair claimed the leadership of the stonemason guilds of Scotland, which resulted in major political intrigue between his allies and the allies of Sir William Alexander. I tell this story in more detail in a future chapter as it is central not only to the theories in this book, but also to the foundation of Freemasonry.

The case of George Home, assistant to his son William Jr., is another good example of William Sr.'s power.

Home was essentially an outlaw when Sir William Alexander hired him to solicit settlers in Scotland, and to gather supplies for the voyage to Nova Scotia.

What was behind his outlawry was that he owed a serious amount of money to William Watt, a London merchant whose father was John Watt, one of the founders of the East India Company, and the former Sheriff and later, Mayor of London.

John Watt was knighted on July 26, 1603, at which time he was oddly described in a letter to the king of Spain as "...the greatest pirate that has ever been in this kingdom."

It has to be remembered that all over Europe there were outlaws of all stripes – the powerful, the lackeys of the powerful, and the broken men, who had no other choice but thievery. The *Register of the Privy Council of Scotland*, where I have found so much valuable information (this after hours and hours of reviewing and translating into words that are more modern and understandable) is rife with lawsuits and charges being filed between the powerful and the peasants. And this is only what made it into the Privy Council records!

Across Scotland, at the time of the Baronets of Nova Scotia, there were crimes being committed on all sides, virtually every hour of the day. There was no industrial revolution to employ the broken men, and not enough farmland to go around. The roads were haunted by highwaymen, and the alleys of the larger cities with even worse. Part of the goal of the Baronets adventure was, in fact, to provide another choice for men who were willing to take a chance on Nova Scotia.

A plaque displayed at Annapolis Royal states that "most of the Scots settlers left Nova Scotia" in 1632, but it doesn't say that they all did. Another record indicates that two Scots stayed behind because they had married Mi'kmaq spouses. Baronet George Home may have stayed behind for another reason altogether – a reason that included witchcraft and warrants for his arrest.

William Alexander Jr. left Nova Scotia in 1630. He put Sir George Home of Manderston in charge of the settlers there. George was once a well-to-do country gentleman who had married into wealth. He arranged for his wife to partition off part of her property in the name of his son Alexander, with the caveat that she would control ownership of the land for the balance of her life.

Both George and his son Alexander had been knighted and seemed to be upstanding men – that is until George's debts began to grow. His wife soon realized that she would likely lose her right to the land if it was sold to pay off George's debts. This was, in fact, George's plan, and apparently his only option.

She chased George out of the house and threatened his undoing if he didn't leave her estate alone. He, in turn, accused her of witchcraft.

One Alexander Hamilton was, at the time, being accused of being a warlock. It was common for people like him, who were typically falsely accused, to accuse others in hopes of leniency. Hamilton was imprisoned at the Old Tolbooth in Edinburgh, where George Home was one of the men who took down his testimony against the others.

One of the "others" accused was Mrs. George Home, otherwise known as Lady Manderston, George's own wife. The husband and wife were known to be on bad terms, and the charge that Hamilton brought against the lady was that she used "devilish practices" against the life of her husband. When specifically interrogated, Hamilton admitted that his only grounds for making the charge was a statement of one John Neil, of Tweedmouth. Hamilton was "sent to his account," but his informant, John Neil, was carefully looked after and lodged in the Tolbooth of Edinburgh, at least for awhile.

In March of 1631, a case occurs which throws some light upon an affair in which Sir George Home of Manderston was purported to be the intended victim.

John Neil, of Tweedmouth, was then brought forward and tried for sorcery and witchcraft. Among other bad deeds, he was charged with "meeting with the devil and other witches at Coldingham Law, and consulting how Sir George Home of Manderston might be destroyed, to that end getting ane enchanted dead foal, and putting it in Sir George's stable, under his horse's manger and putting a dead hand enchanted by the devil in Sir George's garden in Berwick; by which enchantments Sir George contracted a grievous disease, of which he could not be recovered till the said foal and hand were discovered and bunt (blunted or cleared)."

John Neil was found guilty.

Though the accusation didn't cause Lady Manderston much difficulty, it did buy time for George Home to work at relieving his debt load, and to aid Sir William Alexander in making arrangements for the voyage to Nova Scotia.

George and his son Alexander received protection from the king to travel to Scotland to resolve legal issues, and in George's case, to gather settlers and supplies for William Alexander. He may have felt, in the middle of this insanity, that Nova Scotia was a better place to be.

His protection issued by King Charles I is recorded in the Privy Council minutes in this fashion:

Forsameekle as the Kings Majestie being informed that there hes beene some devilish practises of witchecraft used by certane persouns aganis Sir George Home of Manderstoun, his Majestie has beene pleased by his letter direct to the Lords of Secreit Counsell to signifie his will and pleasure for a protectioun to be grantit to the said Sir Greorge to the intent he may repaire in publict for the better cleering of the truthe of that bussines; thairfoir the Lords of Secreit Counsell according to the practising directioun of his Majesteis said letter, whilk wes this day exhibite before him thame, hes givin and grantit, and be the tennour heirof gives and grants libertie and warrand to the said Sir George Home for his saulffe repaire in the countrie without danger of the law for the purpose and to the effect above writtin untill the twentie day of Januarie next, discharging in the meane tyme all shireffs, Stewarts, bailleis of regaliteis, and their deputs, provests and bailleis within burgh, and all others his Majesteis Judges, officiars, and mistrats, to burgh and land, and als all officiars of armes, of all taking, apprehending, warding or arresting of the said Sir George.

This got George off the hook for awhile, but evidence seems to indicate that he never did come back to Scotland to settle his debts. Another record shows a supplication by Sir George Home, as follows – "Sir William Alexander has 'imployed him in some charge anent the plantation of Nova Scotia' and sent him to Scotland to list men and provide victuals, and other things necessary therefor. He is here to follow out the same, but some of his creditors threaten him with horning, so that he cannot go about his duties without licence from their Lordships. This he therefore craves."

"Horning" meant requiring a debtor to pay his debts or be branded a rebel. Home was eventually branded a rebel and warrants were issued for his arrest. The last we hear of him, in Privy Council records, is when his son makes a bid for freedom to return to Scotland to sell their land to pay the family's debts, and states that his father cannot return to this land because he is branded a rebel. I could find no further information on George Home except for one record that said he died in 1636.

It is at least possible that this co-leader of the Scots of Nova Scotia decided to stay right where he was, safe from witches and warrants.

Alexander family records state that John Alexander, grandson of the man who formed the Baronets of Nova Scotia, also stayed behind at New Ross, just 20 miles or so from Oak Island, and that William Alexander Jr., who led the Port Royal Scots, died in Nova Scotia, in 1638.

Another Scot who stayed behind was the Alexander-related wife of Claude de la Tour, Baronet of Nova Scotia and ally of William Alexander who owned the coastline from Yarmouth to Lunenburg. It has been said that she was offered safe passage back to Scotland, but refused, deciding instead to remain with her husband, a man who also died about 1636.

This shows that Alexander family interest in the area nearby Oak Island remained strong, even after 1632.

Here's a question – If the Coat of Arms for Nova Scotia (shown above), and the very name of Nova Scotia, both date from 1621 through 1632, then why couldn't the mystery of Oak Island also date from 1632, due to the reluctant exodus of these Scots from their home in New Scotland?

Chapter Five
PORT ROYAL

A lot had to happen before William Alexander was willing to send his son off to Nova Scotia. As stated earlier, it was a request from the Pilgrims of Plymouth, Massachusetts, that sparked an attempt to chase out the final few French settlers from Acadia (or what became known as Nova Scotia) after the settlement at Port Royal was attacked by Captain Argall, in 1613.

King James I of England and Ireland (King James VI of Scotland) was faced with a dilemma as to how to placate these British settlers so that others might follow them to populate New England. He naturally turned to his long-time advisor and friend Sir William Alexander for a plan.

Alexander came up with the brilliant idea that if Scots could be convinced that they could create a New Scotland in Acadia, many would be eager to jump on the bandwagon. The king was more than happy to turn the whole project over to William.

However, William was wrong about one thing. It turned out to be very difficult to convince quality settlers – those with skills in smithing, farming, etc, – to sign up. Oh, there were plenty of broken men ready to go, but what kind of settlers would they make?

In addition, it was necessary to fund this project, procuring ships and supplies.

James I chartered Nova Scotia to William Alexander in 1621, describing New Scotland as – "which lands aforesaid, in all time to come, shall enjoy the name of Nova Scotia, in America."

The actual charter was written in Latin and so New Scotland was spelled Nova Scotia. When the charter was translated into English, the Nova Scotia name remained, and has remained until this very day 396 years later.

At the same time, a Coat of Arms was created for this new land. Though it has been illustrated in a variety of ways and levels of quality, it has remained basically the same for 396 years as well.

My question remains – If the name and the Coat of Arms of Nova Scotia date back to the settlement of Nova Scotia by William Alexander's Scots adventurers, why wouldn't that be an ideal time period to look for clues as to what happened on Oak Island?

I do just that in this book, however, first I need to set the stage a little.

By 1622, Alexander was in firm control of the attempt at a New Scotland. He sent out an exploration ship to see what Nova Scotia was like. However, this ship was beaten back to Newfoundland by a storm and several of its crew were put ashore there while the ship returned to England, where William Alexander now lived. Despite his extensive Scottish connections and upbringing, he continued to own Menstrie Castle, but, because of his government duties, he needed to live in London.

William Alexander unfortunately learned little from this 1622 voyage except that his adventure was likely to get very expensive to undertake.

In 1623, Sir William sent another ship. When it reached Newfoundland, the captain found that several men from the first crew had died. Others were gone fishing somewhere, and so the ten remaining crew members who were left at the settlement climbed aboard this second ship and they all began a voyage down the coast of Nova Scotia, pulling into several bays and studying the land. They recorded, in detail, what they found.

When this second ship returned to England, later that year, they came with exciting news about the possibilities for a great settlement in Nova Scotia.

Alexander then had advertising pieces printed singing the praises of joining in on the adventure. Still, many were reluctant to go and it took five more years just to get enough settlers to make it worthwhile.

Meanwhile, Alexander hit on another idea. He would sell baronies in Nova Scotia to well-to-do men who would receive a fair amount of land for each barony, but would also be required to produce a handful of settlers.

What force was behind the success of this idea is still unclear, however, as I have pointed out, many of the earliest men to sign on were leaders of substantial clans in Scotland – clans who had ties to the old Knights Templar traditions, and even to Sir Henry Sinclair, himself. It could have been as simple as a longing for the good old days of Scotland perhaps to be found in a New Scotland, free from English influence.

Or, it could have been something much deeper. It could have been seen as an opportunity to spirit out of Scotland treasures and artifacts that were destined to stay hidden forever, or worse, to be confiscated in an English-controlled Scotland.

In my book *Oak Island Missing Links,* I identify two items that have been missing from Scotland for centuries that, if found today, would be invaluable. One is the Stone of Destiny, or coronation chair of the Scottish kings. The other is the *Scotichronicon,* or *Chronicles of Scotland,* which was a national history book painstakingly collected and rewritten from many sources throughout Scotland and Ireland, following an end to the English domination of Scotland in the 15th century.

I am not going to revisit my theory about these items, but I suggest that if the reader is interested in learning more about them, they can do so by reading my previous book *Oak Island Missing Links.*

In addition to the possibility of one or both of these items being taken to Nova Scotia, we are also faced with the fact that the Knights Templar, the wealthiest and most worldly organization in the western world, would have had to disseminate their wealth and artifacts in some fashion that would remain hidden from their enemies, particularly the kings of Europe and the Pope.

In Scotland, the Templars had a friend in King Robert the Bruce. Some of their properties were joined with the Knights of St. John. Others perhaps fell into the hands of Scottish clans who had Knights Templar, Baronets of Nova Scotia, and Freemasons in their history.

If New Scotland, or Nova Scotia, was being looked upon as a new beginning in the long Scottish march for freedom, it is entirely possible that many valuable items were spirited there on ships carrying a safe passage letter from King Charles I.

And, since the Baronets of Nova Scotia roster was filled with clan chieftains, they may have felt that they were ultimately in control of what would happen to these valuable items. After all, they were sending their own clansmen to become settlers there. And they likely anticipated that the colony would grow quickly with the support of the king, and with a highly-placed official like Sir William Alexander leading the way.

Alexander chose Sir George Home to be in charge of lining up the supplies and settlers, perhaps because he was desperate to earn some money to pay his debts and clear his name. Whether George ever believed his wife was a witch, or was just using that story as an excuse, at least working for Sir William was giving him cover, through a Royal mandate, from harassment by his angry creditors – a respite, as it were, from reality, and a chance to participate in a utopian enterprise, instead.

In 1625, Sir William Alexander created the Baronets of Nova Scotia scheme, with the blessings and a charter issued by King James I, who died just four days later.

The son of James I took the throne as Charles I and reiterated his support for the Baronet program.

Over the next three years, leaders and settlers from many Scottish clans signed on. As the money came in, Alexander refined his plans for Nova Scotia.

Still, the costs for this adventure were rising.

For one thing, the *Morning Star*, docked in Scotland, was restricted from leaving port because of debts that were due. Alexander had to spend money to free her up. He also had to supply the ships with enough food, ammunition, and daily survival tools to get the Port Royal Scots through the first couple of winters.

It has been said that over two hundred cows were purchased to make the trip across the ocean. Plus, each ship would need a crew, and there were medals to be made and ceremonies to be held, as each Baronet was installed. The title given to these men was actually Knight Baronet of Nova Scotia, and a medal attached to an orange ribbon was presented to each participant.

Since it was impossible to take possession (or sasine) of a Baronet's property across the ocean, a small area of land at Edinburgh Castle was designated as part of Nova Scotia and the Baronets would go there to receive their medal and claim their barony.

By August 1628, all was set for the voyage, and four ships sailed from the Isle of Man for Nova Scotia. If reports are to be believe, one of the privateers commanded by David Alexander had a change of heart and pursued a ship from another country, first leaving their Nova Scotia-bound settlers off on the shores of Scotland.

Sailing about the same time were ships under the direction of Sir Robert Gordon, who was given Cape Breton, and also ships under the direction of five brothers known by the surname Kirk, who managed to capture some French ships along the way.

The Kirk brothers' focus was on the entire east coast of Canada, not so much on the province of Nova Scotia. They were reasonably successful in their adventure, until they, too, had to leave Canada, in 1632. Gordon's group left before then, as they were chased out of Cape Breton by the French, after just a short stay.

William Alexander's group, led by his son William Alexander Jr., never made it to Port Royal that year. Instead, they were blown by a storm to Newfoundland, where they spent the winter.

With the Alexander company now stranded at Newfoundland, the Kirk brothers petitioned the king to let them take over the settlement of Nova Scotia. On November 18, 1628, the Kirk petition was fought against by several upstanding men from England and Scotland requesting that the king allow Sir William Alexander to continue in his quest.

Their supplication stated, in part that going back on his word to Alexander would:

...prove so derogatorie to this your ancient kingdome, under the great seale whereof your Majestie lies alreadie granted a right to the saids bounds, and will so exceedinglie discourage all undertakers of that kynde, as we cannot but at their humble sute represent the same to your Majestie; humblie intreatting that your Majestie may be graciouslie pleased to take this into your princelie consideratioun as no right may be heereafter graunted of the saids lands contrarie to your Majesteis said preceiding graunt, but that they may be still holdin of the crowne of this your ancient kingdome, according to the

purport and trew intentioun of your Majesteis said former graunt. And we ar verie hopefull that, as the said Sir Williame Alexander hes sent furth his soune with a colonie to plant there this last yeere, so it saal be secunded heerafter by manie other undertakers of good worth for the advancement of your Majesteis service, increasse of your revenewes, and honnour of this your said ancient kingdome. (Privy Council Register)

In other words, they were saying that, if the king went back on his promises, it would be impossible to organize anymore settlement efforts in the New World, because the settlers would not trust the king's word.

This was enough to convince Charles I, if he needed any convincing at all, to leave things as they were.

William Jr. returned to England in the fall of 1628 to get more supplies. In his absence, 30 settlers died. When he returned to Newfoundland, the Scots sailed on to Port Royal, establishing a settlement there on April 23, 1629, which lasted almost exactly three years.

William Jr. made another trip to England, returning in 1630, and bringing with him the former leader of the French at Port Royal. His name was Claude de la Tour, and he'd been captured by the Kirk brothers in 1629.

In England, Claude had made peace with Sir William Alexander and Charles I, and actually married one of the Queen's handmaidens, who happened to be a relative of William Alexander. In return, he and his son were given honorary Baronet of Nova Scotia grants.

Claude's land extended from present-day Yarmouth to Lunenburg, a town not too distant from Oak Island.

Claude's son, Charles, had already established a fort on Cape Sable Island and when his father approached the island with the honorary Baronet title, Charles de la Tour chased him away. For two days Claude attempted to forcibly take the Cape Sable Island fort, but was unsuccessful. Finally, he resigned himself that his son would remain loyal to France, while he enjoyed the fruits of his alliance with England.

From the book *Memorials of the Earl of Stirling and of the House of Alexander, Volume 1* we've learned several things about Sir William's adventure in Nova Scotia. One sections reads:

In the autumn of 1629, Claude de la Tour, the former Governor of Port Royal under the French, visited England. Introduced at court, he married as his second wife, one of the Queen's maids of honor. (It has been reported in several books that this woman was kin to Sir William Alexander.) *On the 30th of November he received a patent as a Baronet of New Scotland; and on the payment of a sum of money, obtained from Sir William Alexander, a grant of territory extending from the sea inland thirty or forty miles, and reaching from the site of the present Yarmouth north-easterly to Lunenburg. In accepting these lands, Sir Claude bound himself to become a good and faithful subject of the British sovereign. With two ships of war he sailed for New Scotland in May 1630 and landed at Cape Sable. To his son Charles, who commanded the French garrison at Cape Sable, he offered a patent of Baronetcy, with a commission authorizing his continuance in office, on his submitting to British rule.*

Indignant at the offer he (Charles de la Tour) *rejected the proposal and offered to defend the fort with his life. Returning to his ship Sir Claude again affectionately entreated his son to surrender himself. Meeting a second refusal, Sir Claude landed his men. For two days he attacked the fort, but was compelled to return to his ship.*

The two sides, father and son, managed to live peacefully beside each other in the vast Nova Scotian wilderness, but never were able to make amends. The mother of Charles de la Tour had died long before their voyage to Acadia, and perhaps he couldn't accept that his father was remarried to another woman – an English woman at that.

Whatever the reason, Charles de la Tour remained aloof, and doesn't enter the picture again until 1654, when he accepts the inheritance of his father's land, granted to him by Oliver Cromwell, then immediately sells it to two Englishmen in order to pay off his debts.

Although the Scots evacuation had left Nova Scotia to the French, in 1632, this action by Charles de la Tour gave England a new excuse to claim that land. Of course, a lot would happen in between 1632 and 1654.

To begin with, Charles I, who chartered the Baronets of Nova Scotia, was married to a French noblewoman named Henriette Maria, who was the youngest daughter of Henry IV, King of France. The State of Maryland was named for her. His brother-in-law was now King of France, as Louis XIII. Louis had gained the throne at a young age, after his father was assassinated.

The two brothers-in-law were finally trying to get along after having been at war over the last few years.

France still owed Charles I the second half of a dowry from his marriage to his French princess. He had gone in debt to a substantial degree and this dowry money would put him right with most of his debtors. But Louis, his own brother-in-law, was delaying payment.

About the same time, Charles' agent, Sir William Alexander, was claiming land that had already been claimed by France as Acadia. His son William Jr. had even been given a commission to capture French ships, which may be why the two ships set to accompanied the *Eagle* and *Morning Star* were the privateers, the *James* and the *Alexander*, both led by David Alexander.

Once they had permission to take ships from Spain or France, the *Alexander* almost immediately captured two French ships just previous to the trip to Nova Scotia.

William Alexander Jr. was busy as well. A pinnace (a small boat with sails or oars forming part of the equipment of a larger vessel) was taken from the French and carried to England. Also, a ship called the *Mary of St Jean de Luz*, of seventy tons burthen, was captured by Alexander. The port of St. Jean de Luz, in southern France, was known as the "viper's nest" by British sailors because of its notorious Basque pirates.

Though it may not have been Charles' original intent, Nova Scotia became a bargaining chip with Louis XIII.

From a letter by Charles I written to the Privy Council we learn that the French government had raised a claim to Acadia, where Sir William Alexander had sought to plant his Scottish colony. The contention of France was that the lands had been seized during the late war between the two countries, and, now that peace was restored, it had a right to claim its own. That he might be prepared to answer this demand, Charles I asked the Council to supply him with precise information regarding the claims of Scotland to the land in question.

As the beginning of the rivalry between France and Britain for the possession of Canada, this early dispute had an additional element of trouble for each country.

The threatened visit of a plague at the close of 1629 called for some type of action from the Council. The plague was described as "the contagious sickness of the pest," and was especially prevalent in Bordeaux, France, and in the Orkney and Shetland Islands of Scotland.

The Privy Council of King Charles imposed a rigorous quarantine in connection with Scottish ports, but from the repeated ordinances it passed, it is evident that it received only partial obedience.

Both countries had their challenges, and both had something to gain by the discontinuance of the Baronets of Nova Scotia program.

Though progress was being made at Port Royal, reached by the Scots in the summer of 1629, the French weren't giving up so easily.

In January of 1629, a statement had been laid before the English government, which read: "The King of France, by his commissions, doeth assure to himself all that part of America... whereby he doeth incluid the River of Canada, all Acady (Acadia), etc."

On April 23, 1629, a treaty of peace was signed between France and England, in which it was provided that, though prizes taken during the war should be retained by the captors, whatever was seized on either side, for two months after the signing of the peace, should be restored. This meant Port Royal belonged to the French according to the treaty. However, William Jr. appears to have arrived there on that very same day!

So much had gone into this venture, so much money along with the reputation of the Alexander family had been invested, that the Scots were not willing to give up on Port Royal.

Unfortunately for Charles I, he found himself needing to play both sides of the field, keeping his French brother-in-law happy by signing a treaty returning Nova Scotia to the French, while reassuring the many Scottish and some English noblemen (including his good friend and advisor William Alexander) who had all invested so much in the adventure. He told them he had no intention of giving up on the project, and that this was only a temporary setback for the settlement of Nova Scotia, despite the fact that he had signed a peace treaty in which Nova Scotia would be given back to France, if Louis would pay the balance of Charles' dowry.

Despite the king's reassurance, in July 1631, the Scots of Port Royal were informed that they would soon need to leave. Many resisted the idea and there was no immediate movement to vacate their settlement.

There was also a short delay in that Charles I insisted that the dowry funds be completely paid before he would instruct the Scots to leave. This bought them a bit more time in Nova Scotia. Meanwhile, the order for the Scots to evacuate was sent to the French in Quebec to be held until the final date of transfer, which was to be March 29, 1632.

From all available evidence, 300 French soldiers from Quebec descended upon Port Royal about March 25, 1632, to inform the Scots living there that they would need to leave.

There has been a long-standing tradition that the Scots were commanded to tear down their fort at the first of the year, which would normally be around January 1st.

I had wondered since reading this – If this was part of a peace treaty, why would the Scots have been treated so poorly in the middle of a cold Nova Scotian winter, and also where did they live until the March 29th deadline that they were given to begin their departure?

I believe I have found these answers, based on the calendar customs of England from that time period.

The new year didn't begin on January 1st in England, back in 1632. In fact, it wasn't until 1752 that January 1st began to be used. There are many old records in the British Isles that list events, such as death notices and other legal documents as, for example, "2 February 1622-23," the reason being that the said February was in 1622, using the old system, but in 1623, using the new.

The accepted beginning of any new year took place on March 25th, in this case just four days before the forced evacuation of the Scots from Port Royal.

Sir William wrote to the king that the French enacted the evacuation "immediately upon the late treaty."

On the 16th of June, Sir William Alexander submitted to the king the following note (written here in more modern, understandable English):

A minute of some points considerable for his Majesty's service in regard of the French their possessing of New Scotland at this time. The possessing of it by the French immediately upon the late treaty (on March 29, 1632), though it be not warranted by the treaty, if some speedy act do not disprove it, will be held to be authorized by it.

He further states: "They have this year sent 300 men to New Scotland."

And so it appears that the Scots were, in fact, forced to tear down their fort at the beginning of the year, but a year that began on March 25th, not January 1st.

The treaty may have factored in that it would take the 300 French troops from Quebec about four days to make the trip to Port Royal, to explain to the Scots the rules of the evacuation, and have them tear down their fort, so that, on the appointed day of March 29th, the evacuation proceedings could begin.

The actual order for the evacuation reads:

The said term of eight days being given them to retire from said places, positions, and forts, with their arms, baggage, goods, gold, silver, furniture, and generally all that may belong to them – to whom and to all those who are in said places is given a term of three weeks after the said eight days are expired, during which, or sooner, if may be, to embark in

*their vessels with their arms – and generally all which belongs
to them, to remove from thence into England without staying
longer in those countries.*

All indications are that, on March 29, 1632, the Scots
were given eight days to pack their belongings and three
additional weeks to actually set sail. This was obviously
not a war-like move or they simply would have been
taken prisoner or possibly killed, and at the very least
their weapons and their gold and silver would have
been confiscated.

Eight days of packing plus three weeks, or 21 days to
sail, would add up to 29 days total to evacuate Port
Royal. This would mean the Scots would need to leave
port on or before April 27, 1632, at a time when the
stormy North Atlantic could have been quite difficult to
sail, due to gale force winds, extremely high waves, and
freezing spray. According to my theory, this is when the
link to the Oak Island mystery really begins.

I feel that from 1632 onward, perhaps throughout the
rest of the 1600s, families associated with the Baronets of
Nova Scotia, who had also become the world's first
Freemasons, continued their interest in Oak Island, and
in the area that became New Ross, as shown by family
records and land grants.

Agatha Campbell, granddaughter of Charles de la
Tour, and wife of a man that I believe descended from
Glooscap, or Gylascop Campbell (and who was also
associated with the Baronets of Nova Scotia) settled the
final claim to Baronet land in 1733, over 100 years later.

The above battlefield at Annapolis Royal, Nova Scotia, evolved from the 1605 French settlement of Port Royal, which was renamed in honor of Queen Anne following the Siege of Port Royal in 1710 by Britain. It was here that Scots settlers maintained a colony from 1629 through 1632, until ousted by an Anglo-French treaty. On March 29, 1632, they were given eight days to pack and three additional weeks to leave, putting them out into the open, and likely very stormy North Atlantic, leading to my theory that they pulled into Mahone Bay, on the opposite side of Nova Scotia, for protection from the weather, taking shelter behind Oak Island.

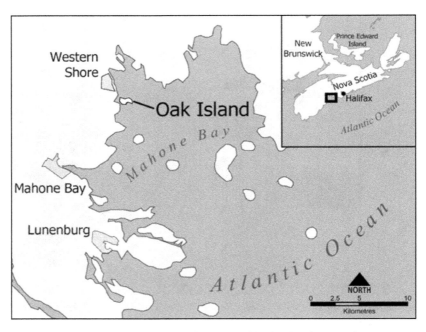

Above is a simple map of the location of Oak Island as it relates to Mahone Bay and the present-day town of Lunenburg. (Wikipedia)

Chapter Six
OAK ISLAND

As can easily be seen, by viewing the map shown on the opposite page, that Oak Island is located on a straight shot towards the back of Mahone Bay, which would make it perhaps the safest place to take refuge in the middle of a North Atlantic storm. In fact, while visiting the Centre of Geographic Sciences, in Lawrencetown, NS, in June of 2017, I was told that there is said to be a direct tack for sailboats from the open ocean to Oak Island.

Oak Island happens to be one of the islands located at the back of Mahone Bay. A 20th century charting of the waters around Oak Island, carried out by a U.S. firm, shows these waters, especially between the island and the mainland, to be at least forty feet deep, not too far off shore – certainly deep enough in which to anchor ships from the 17th century.

Also, note Oak Island's proximity to Lunenburg.

Claude de la Tour, ally to the Scots of Port Royal, controlled the land thirty to forty miles inland from present-day Yarmouth up to Lunenburg, through his honorary Baronet of Nova Scotia title and land grant. Oddly, he paid for his Baronet title, but the money was given to him by William Alexander Sr., most likely in an effort to bring peace to the French and Scots.

These two factors, the convenience of Oak Island as a refuge from a storm, and the closeness of Alexander's ally, Claude de la Tour, to Mahone Bay (and therefore to Oak Island), are important to my theory of how and why Scots from Port Royal could end up on Oak Island.

Another element that supports my theory is carbon dating of finished lumber found either in the swamp, in the Money Pit, or in other Oak Island locations.

I'll address the weather first.

On May 10, 2017, I had the idea that I should look up the NOAA weather report for the North Atlantic to get an idea of what the Port Royal Scots might have been facing, when leaving Port Royal on or before April 27th.

What I found was that, at least on this day in 2017, anyone attempting this feat would have been facing waves up to 15 feet, gale force winds of 25-35 knots, dense fog, and severe freezing spray.

I also found a study done in 1993 showing the water in the Bay of Fundy, where Port Royal was located, to be an average of 35 to 40 degrees Fahrenheit. Closer to Mahone Bay the waters measured 25 to 35 degrees Fahrenheit.

Certainly, the ocean wasn't going to freeze, but it was the freezing spray mentioned in the 2017 weather report, and the freezing waters measured in the 1993 report, that would have caused a wooden ship from the 17th century some serious trouble. Crews on today's more modern metal ships often have to use wooden bats to break the ice off the gunwales to prevent the ship from becoming too heavy and sinking. Doing this to a 17th century wooden ship would certainly take its toll.

Add to this the potentially high waves of up to 15 feet, and high winds of up to 35 knots, and it would have been extremely challenging, if not entirely impossible, for a small fleet of ships to embark on a journey across the North Atlantic around the end of April.

Leaving Port Royal through the Bay of Fundy would not have been as challenging, since it is on the leeward side of Nova Scotia, and according to the temperature study, the waters there seem to remain slightly warmer than at Mahone Bay, and above the freezing mark.

If we imagine our fleet of Scottish settlers rounding the lower part of Nova Scotia, near Yarmouth, they may have been suddenly faced with the same type of ocean storm that was hitting the area on May 10, 2017.

Cape Sable Island would not have been a choice for them to take shelter, since Charles de la Tour had a fort there and was not their ally. However, along the coast, his father, Claude de la Tour, would have been eager to provide protection, since he was not only their ally, but was also married to an Alexander-related woman.

Mahone Bay would be the most obvious choice to find refuge, to wait out the weather for a better time to sail back to the British Isles. How many ships were in this fleet is debatable. With a license to capture Spanish and French ships, and with the two war ships that were said to have brought William Alexander Jr. and Claude de la Tour back to Nova Scotia added in, it is conceivable that there were three to four ships, or perhaps more. And, since the Scots were required to take all of their belongings, these ships would likely be heavily laden.

What exactly these ships were laden with is the question. Obviously, there would have been their arms and munitions, personal belongings, and other goods.

According to the order to leave, they were also instructed to take their gold and silver, which indicates that the French were not on a mission to pillage Port Royal, but rather to allow for a peaceful departure.

If, in fact, these Scots had spirited items out of Scotland and England, such as Bacon's manuscripts, Templar treasures now in the hands of Scottish clans, or national treasures of Scotland, like the Stone of Destiny or *Scotichronicon*, it doesn't sound like the French were interested in demanding that they leave anything behind, and, in fact, quite the opposite, were ordering them to take "...all which belongs to them, and remove thence to England..."

The question arises – Would they have wanted to take "all which belongs to them" back to England?

There are at least three reason why they wouldn't.

First, it remained unclear whether the Scots venture was, in fact, destined to fail. The Port Royal Scots may have viewed this departure as simply a bump in the road, and felt it unnecessary to transport everything back to Great Britain, if it was just going to be brought back later that year, or in the following years to come. Some Scots may have even stayed behind to continue the venture.

Secondly, they may have decided to unload some of their items due to the fact that the ships were likely heavily laden, and it would be safer to leave some of their cargo behind, for safety's sake, due to high seas.

Thirdly, they may have been carrying items they did not want people in Great Britain to know about, such as the earlier mentioned Bacon manuscripts, Templar artifacts, or national Scottish treasures. They may have even amassed a fair amount of gold and other treasures from their privateering enterprises carried out by William Alexander Jr., and his relative David Alexander, both on record as having taken several enemy ships as prizes.

Their gold and silver may even have been mined in Nova Scotia, as William Alexander Sr. was specifically given the rights to all mining proceeds.

In the very same section of his 1621 charter for Nova Scotia, where this name first appears in history, the words gold and silver also appear:

Which lands aforesaid, in all time to come, shall enjoy the name of Nova Scotia, in America, which also the aforesaid Sir William shall divide into parts and portions, as to him may seem meet, and give names to the same, according to his pleasure; together with all mines, as well royal of gold and silver, as other mines of iron, lead, copper, brass, tin, and other minerals whatsoever, with power of digging them, and causing them to be dug out of the earth, of purifying and refining the same, and converting and using them to his own proper use, or to other uses whatsoever, as to the said Sir William Alexander, his heirs or assigns, or those whom it shall have happened that he shall have established in his stead, in the said lands, shall seem meet. (Reserving only for us and our successors the tenth part of the metal, commonly called ore of gold and silver, which hereafter shall be dug up or gained.)

It is interesting to note that any gold or silver returned to the British Isle would be taxed at 10%. If it was secretly taken out of its hiding place a little at a time, there would be no taxes to worry about.

It is known that, two centuries later, miners along the Yukon River hid massive amounts of gold from tax collectors, and it is even a theory that Samuel Ball, a freed slave who owned a good chunk of Oak Island, actually paid his debts with old coins, spent a little at a time, that had not likely been taxed by any government agency.

The bottom line is, we cannot be sure exactly what treasures would have been on these ships, but we can be sure that there were some, simply based on the directive towards the Scots to take their gold and silver with them as they left Port Royal.

We also cannot be sure exactly how many ships left Port Royal that day. We can only know about those ships led by the Alexander family that were reported in the Privy Council minutes due to some legal issue, or the ships indicated in other records like those written about in the book *Terror Of The Seas: Scottish Maritime Warfare 1513-1713*, mentioned in Chapter Four of this book.

Even with these records we can't be sure of what took place out on the high seas surrounding Nova Scotia, except that the above-mentioned book states that: "The Scots under Sir William's authority carried the war further than most privateers by actually conducting amphibious operations."

It is likely that the cargo on the flotilla of ships that left Port Royal, on or around April 27, 1632, was extremely valuable, and not something the Scots would like to lose at sea (not to mention along with their own lives).

The safest bet was to pull into the deepest bay around, tack straight back to the most protected island, anchor in sufficiently deep water near that island, enjoying the protection of the island and the protection of your ally. And, why not leave some of this valuable cargo safely behind, until your return, buried in a nine-level Oak Island pit designed to perplex treasure hunters as it has done now for at least 222 years, or perhaps more?

So far, I've shown how the name Nova Scotia and the Coat of Arms of Nova Scotia date back to this same time period I am writing about, which begs the simple question – Why can't the Oak Island mystery date back to this same significant period in Nova Scotian history?

I've shown how the Scots' ships leaving Port Royal were specifically allowed to take all their belongings, including their gold and silver, with them, and could likely have carried any number of unique valuables from Bacon's books, to Templar treasures, to Scottish souvenirs, to privateering prizes, to mined minerals.

Any one or more of the above treasures are possible as shown in the pages of this book. But what specific evidence is there from Oak Island that would support the theory of any of these items being buried there?

Well, surprisingly, there is some evidence.

I have, so far, come across information regarding a few carbon dated items, or historically dating attempts, many of which could place these items within a window of time that could include 1632.

For instance, on March 6, 1981, a stake submitted by the treasure hunters of Triton Alliance Ltd. for carbon dating came back with a date of 1700, plus or minus 80 years. This means its carbon dating window could extend from 1620 through 1780.

A wood slat, also submitted by Triton, was tested two days earlier with a date of 1670, plus or minus 70 years, giving it a window of 1600 through 1740.

Admittedly, these are huge windows of carbon dating for these items. But they do allow for the 1632 date.

In 1969, a group called T'ang Management sent in three pieces of wood from a dig on Oak Island for carbon dating. Two were too small to date, but the third dated to 1575, plus or minus 85 years. This would mean a window of 1490 to 1660, again allowing for the 1632 date.

It would be hard to understand how there could be items buried in or around 1575, and then additional items buried even as late as 1780. It is more likely that all this finished lumber was created and used during the same burial of items on Oak Island, in the 1600s.

In the Oak Island Museum at the Atlantica Resort, which is located very near Oak Island, there is a photo of wood and cement samples found at a depth of 196 feet. These carbon dated to 1595, plus or minus 75 years. This would leave a window of 1520 to 1670, again allowing for the 1632 date.

More recently, on the *Curse of Oak Island* TV show, a few finished lumber pieces were dated in and around the late 1600s, with a smaller window of plus or minus 25 years. If the more common plus or minus of 70 to 85 years was used, these items would also fit nicely into a time frame that could include the year 1632.

Fred Nolan found 60 old spruce stakes in the swamp, along with many other ship parts. These stakes were described in a well-known article, written by Virginia Morell, called "The Pit & The Perplexities," back in 1983. At the time, Nolan acknowledged that, "That entire swamp is man made, just like the beach as Smith's Cove. I don't know why yet, but with time, I think I will."

One theory says that a ship sank in that area before it was a swamp. The idea is currently fairly prevalent that a dam was built to contain the elements of the ship from washing out to sea, either to hide the fact that it was there, or to protect whatever the ship was carrying.

The stakes Nolan found are described in the article as – "...two and one-half to three feet in length, about four inches in diameter at the top and whittled down to a narrow two-inch peg. He found them pounded deep into a swampy area on his part of the island."

Nolan stated, "They were hammered almost all the way into the ground, so that just the little round circles of the top were showing. As I found each one, I marked its location on a chart of the island. If you line these points up, they intersect in some curious ways."

The author of the article then remarks, "Nolan gave another grin but would say no more."

Nolan did state that the stakes carbon dated to just before 1700. Applying a typical plus or minus to this date would put these stakes also in a carbon dating crossover window that would include 1632.

These stakes need to be explored further. From what was said in the article, they were made of spruce, about 30 inches long, identical in shape, and were "whittled" from four inches at the top down to a two inch "peg" at the bottom. Nolan described the "little round circles of the top." They apparently were not sharpened.

Spruce wood is known to have been the wood of choice for most tall ship builders of that day. Trunks of the spruce tree made perfect masts, since they grew very straight. The wood was lightweight, easily cut and worked, and the spruce pitch was even used to seal joints.

One idea for the purpose of these stakes could be that they were a very early version of a ship's rigging known as belaying pins. Modern belaying pins are very refined and made of hardwood or metal. But, since they were just then being invented in the 1600s, they could possibly have been made from spruce in some cases, and could have looked like Fred's "stakes."

If not an early form of belaying pin, the stakes still present a puzzle since they were found all the way down into the ground and were not connected to other pieces of wood, discounting the likelihood that they were part of a fence or a dock.

To the right is a photograph of a stake found by Fred Nolan, provided by the folks at Oak Island. It has been digitally adjusted to approximate the description and the proportions of the stakes that were mentioned in the magazine article.

It has been said that Fred Nolan locked away these stakes and his accompanying paperwork.

What other clues do we have?

In one season of *Curse of Oak Island* a long plank was found in the swamp that appears to have possibly come from the deck or the side of a ship. Considering the number of years it laid in the swamp, it was in relatively good condition. Carbon dating for the plank gives a range of 1680 to 1735 as the age of the plank, using a plus or minus of 25 years.

If the earlier factor of plus or minus 70-80 years was applied, this plank would fall into the 1632 time period.

Wood is given a plus or minus, not so much because carbon dating can't be more accurate, but because it can't be known when the wood was cut down. It could have been cut or have fallen in a storm and not used as a finished lumber piece for another 70 to 80 years before it would start showing signs of dry rot. So, at least in the past, wood was given a wide plus or minus range to account for this unknown factor.

Also, a deck nail was found. It was verified by two experts. One of the people verifying the nail was Gary Drayton, who has discovered hundreds of such nails on 17th century shipwrecks in Florida. It was later verified as a deck nail by an independent antiquities expert.

In addition, several years back a boatswain's whistle was found on an Oak Island beach. Historically, the boatswain's whistle was used to pass commands to the crew when the voice could not be heard over the sounds of the sea. Because of its high pitch, it could be heard over the activities of the crew and in bad weather. And bad weather is exactly the reason why I believe the Port

Royal fleet chose to, or were forced to take shelter near Oak Island. It is entirely possible that one of their ships was too damaged to continue and was scuttled with its cargo in the small cove that became the swamp, or simply was driven into the swamp or cove area by the storm, and there it sank, treasure and all.

It appears a coffer dam was built to contain whatever was lost there, perhaps during recovery efforts.

That a ship could have been forced into this cove was proven over the 2016-17 winter when the road along the swamp was nearly washed out. At great expense, a new road was built between the swamp and the sea using many tons of boulders and gravel. Without this man-made dam and road, and with the cove open to the sea, any ship trying desperately to find shelter along the coast of Oak Island could have easily wash into the cove and sank there.

The fact that ship items have been found in the swamp, and that a man-made coffer dam was built in the distant past shows that the scenario of a ship, perhaps from the fleet of the Port Royal Scots, was either shipwrecked or scuttled in the cove, and then, to contain and recover its contents, a dam was built across the mouth of the cove.

The questions remain – What is the alternative explanation as to why ship items were found in the cove/ swamp? And why was the cove originally partitioned off to create a swamp in the first place? There doesn't seem to be any other reasonable explanation for this evidence, and it is being considered, more and more, as the true history of the swamp.

If a ship from the Port Royal Scots was damaged heavily in the storm, it may have tried to take shelter in the cove and ended up sinking there. If they then decided to stash items from that ship, or items they simply did not want to take back to Great Britain with them, they may have buried them in the Money Pit, or elsewhere on Oak Island or the nearby mainland, thus directly linking items found in the swamp to items found in the Money Pit, and in other locations.

The 300-year-old, or perhaps older, Spanish-style scissors found on the beach could be explained in that we know these Scots were commissioned to capture any French or Spanish ships they came across.

One piece of evidence that is puzzling is the Spanish coin found in the swamp. The date is said to read 1652.

It was in 1654, just two years later, that Oliver Cromwell made the deal with Charles de la Tour to approve his inheritance of his father's claim to Nova Scotia through his Baronet title, so that it could be sold back to two Englishmen for the costs of de la Tour's debts.

In 1659, it appears John Alexander left the New Ross area under pressure from Oliver Cromwell's troops. His son, Alexander Alexander, is said to have been born at New Ross, just 20 miles or so from Oak Island.

Recently, additional English coins dating to the late 1600s were found, along with part of another Spanish coin from the 1600s. These and earlier finds, along with carbon dated finished lumber seem to point to the 1600s as being a period of considerable activity on and/or near Oak Island.

I don't mean to argue with the opinion of the man who cleaned and identified the Spanish coin. In looking at the superimposed date of 1652, it does seem to be what is on the coin. Below is a very enlarged photo of the coin image with the 1652 date superimposed on it, as shown on *Curse of Oak Island*.

In the actual words of the coin reviewer "It's really hard to make it out." He then added that he was "pretty sure" about the date. Below is the same coin with the date 1612 superimposed over the image. Without holding the actual coin in my hand, it at least appears that either date might possibly work.

Meanwhile, I'll take the word of the folks at Oak Island that it is, in fact, from 1652.

It is no wonder that the date is hard to read, appearing smashed or contorted, as this copper coin spent well over 300 years in a brackish swamp, and who knows how worn it was when it was deposited there? The point is simply that it is so worn, it may be impossible to date it accurately, other than that it was from the 1600s.

If it was from 1612, it would certainly fit into my theory of the 1632 shipwreck and Money Pit burial. If it is from 1652, then I can only explain its presence due to Scots working at a later date on Oak Island. We know the last Alexanders were living nearby, at New Ross, until about 1659. Other coins found in Season Five of *Curse of Oak Island*, appear to be from the later 1600s, as well.

None of this takes away from the fact that many ship-related items were found in the swamp, and it is likely we don't even know yet about all of them.

It has been said that Fred Nolan did find other ship parts in the swamp, and so it seems likely that a ship sank there, or was purposely scuttled there, when the swamp was a cove open to the ocean.

There is always the possibility that the ship was a Spanish ship, scuttled to hide its existence, and with its treasure buried in the Money Pit. This ship could have been taken by the Scots of Port Royal since they had a commission from the king encouraging them to do so.

It could even have been the Basque ship *Mary of St Jean de Luz* that we know was captured by William Alexander Jr.

St. Jean de Luzis was located very near the border between France and Spain, and the Basque people seem to straddle both French and Spanish cultures.

This could explain the Spanish style scissors found on the beach, the deck nail from the swamp, which Gary Drayton said matched those he'd found on Spanish shipwrecks down around Florida, the Spanish coin, and even the piece of Spanish jewelry presented by the McGinnes family as being left over from a chest Daniel McGinnes is said to have found in the Money Pit.

Other items found on Oak Island indicate an ancient date for whatever activity took place, pre-Money Pit. These include hand wrought nails, low carbon steel estimated at 300 or more years in age, and an ancient ruler (or perhaps part of a set square).

There have been too many ancient items and too much carbon dated finished lumber from the 1600s, along with ship items in the swamp or on the beach, to doubt that something unique, and perhaps quite dramatic happened on Oak Island.

The ownership of land in Nova Scotia, as relates to the Baronets of Nova Scotia, appears, by all available evidence, to have ranged from 1621, when Nova Scotia was first given to William Alexander, until 1733, when the very last Baronet-related claim to Nova Scotia land was settled.

Baronet titles including land grants were issued until 1638. Baronet titles without land grants continued to be issued until 1706. In both the 1700s and 1800s, Baronets petitioned the king to regain their Nova Scotia land.

There is enough evidence, I believe, to warrant looking at the Scots of Port Royal as having taken refuge on Oak Island, in 1632, perhaps lingering on into the late 1600s, and leaving behind something of value in a nine-level pit that has defied treasure hunters, ever since.

With the past links of Baronets of Nova Scotia to the Knights Templar, and links that followed to the Freemasons, and especially with the link of John Smith, one of the three young men who first dug into the Money Pit (and one of the earliest owners of the Money Pit lot), whose mother was from the Templar and Freemason connected MacLean family, there just seems to be too much coincidence going on, unless it was no coincidence at all.

This final bit of evidence barely made it into this book, it is such a fresh discovery. The area surrounding Mahone Bay, including the town of Lunenburg, was once known as Mirligaiche. While the name is sometimes attributed to the Mi'kmaq, the word is a Scots Gaelic word meaning "part of the link" - *mir* meaning a "piece, part, fragment," and *ligaiche* meaning "link."

What link this refers to, I don't know yet, but what I do know is that in the Baronet charter issued to Claude de la Tour, by Sir William Alexander, in 1630, the lands from Yarmouth to Mirligaiche are specifically given to Claude. An official government document from 1916 says that Mirligaiche included ALL the islands in Mahone Bay. This means that, as of 1630, Claude de la Tour, ally of the Scots settlers of Port Royal, owned Oak Island, two years before I believe these same Scots took refuge there!

Above is a photo of what has been called the "G stone." It was found face down, during a dig at Smith's Cove. The letter G is said to be representative of God, or of the Great Architect, in Masonic lore. Below is a typical Masonic symbol combining a set square, a compass, and the letter G.

Chapter Seven
ENTER THE FREEMASONS

William Alexander Jr. is the man who led the Scots in the settlement of Port Royal, Nova Scotia, under his father's direction, and the king's approval.

William Alexander Jr. was also the first man ever to be named a non-operative, speculative Freemason. He was joined by his brother Anthony, and by Sir Alexander Strachan, another Baronet of Nova Scotia. They were all initiated on the same day – July 3, 1634.

What if I were to tell you, according to all normally accepted stories on the forming of the Freemasons out of the stonemason lodges of Scotland, that, in fact, the first seven Freemasons in history (and even more in later years) were associated with the Baronets of Nova Scotia?

The nine-level Money Pit on Oak Island has been said to be patterned after the Masonic Royal Arch Degree, which also includes nine-levels, and includes three sojourners making their way through these nine levels.

Prolific Oak Island and Nova Scotian author Mark Finnan appears to be the first to draw detailed attention to the links between Freemasonry and the Oak Island legend. Finnan, in the 1997 edition of his book *Oak Island Secrets*, noted that many of the treasure diggers have been Freemasons, and implied that the Masonic fraternity possessed secret knowledge of the nature of the treasure which compelled them to seek it.

Other authors, in articles, books and on the web, have expanded and expounded on the theory that the legend of the Money Pit, and the three young men who discovered it, is somehow driven by Masonic ritual.

What if I told you that I believe the exact opposite is true?

By that I mean – What if the Royal Arch ceremony of Freemasonry was, in fact, driven by pragmatic information imparted to, or held by, the earliest of Freemasons on how to retrieve what was buried in the Money Pit on Oak Island?

And, what if that pragmatic information slowly developed into a ritual instead, because not enough details survived until such a time as any of those in the know could get back to Oak Island to recover the buried items?

And what if I told you that the Masonic rule is that every time the Royal Arch ritual is undertaken, three initiates must be present, and this may be related to the pragmatic fact that three initiates *were* present – as the very first Freemasons in history?

Can pragmatic information develop into ritual over a long period of time? Yes, in fact, there are several examples of this happening.

Marvin Harris, author of the book *Cows, Pigs, Wars, and Witches: The Riddles of Culture*, goes into extensive detail explaining how information or rules based wholly on pragmatic, even mundane, survival can become accepted as some type of unexplainable ritual or belief system, having nothing to do with their original intent.

He tells us, "Another reason why many customs and institutions seem so mysterious is that we have been taught to value elaborate 'spiritualized' explanations of cultural phenomenon more than down-to-earth material ones. I contend that the solution to each of the riddles examined in this (his) book lies in a better understanding of practical circumstances."

He uses the "sacred cow" cultural phenomenon of India as one of his first examples, although he provides many other examples, as well.

The sacred cow culture in India began as a pragmatic approach to a very real problem.

In the past, most families owned only one cow, if they were lucky. If that cow was killed during a time of hunger, there would be no future milk production, and no further oxen production. Oxen were typically the only means for transportation, or for plowing, and cows obviously were needed to give birth to oxen.

With a dearth of available cows in this land, a pragmatic rule was instituted that no family should kill their cow, even if they felt they were starving. This practical ruling has led, over the centuries, to a "spiritualized" view of what some call "cow love."

The author goes on to explain the pragmatic root of many customs, throughout many cultures, that outsiders might look at as bizarre, and yet were born out of a pragmatic need to survive, or to gain power or wealth.

Most early witches, for example, were prosecuted as a way for the ruling class government to avoid any responsibility for the deterioration of their society.

It was much easier to blame a few hundred old, helpless women, rather than have the king or his cronies own up to the fact that they were not solving their country's supply shortages, violence, or sickness.

Personal vendettas were also pursued by making accusations of witchcraft against another person. In the case we've already spoken about, concerning George Home, some historians believe he simply accused his wife of witchcraft in order to hold onto the land he gained by marrying her, and to diffuse the efforts of bill collectors to harass him or have him declared a rebel.

I believe that this is what happened with the Money Pit and the Royal Arch Degree of Freemasonry. I believe that pragmatic knowledge was entered into Freemasonry by the earliest Freemasons in history, about the location of the Money Pit and its contents. Over the years, either to hide this valuable evidence, or simply through misunderstanding, the idea was born that the reverse happened – that the Money Pit was based on Freemasonry ritual, rather than that Freemasonry ritual was based on pragmatic information about the Money Pit.

Two major points to support this theory are: 1) there were no Freemasons anywhere in the world in 1632, and 2) just two years later, the actual leader of the Nova Scotia Scots, along with his brother, and another man who was a Baronet of Nova Scotia, were initiated as the very first Freemasons in history!

The story of the first three Freemasons can be found in several books and in a few online histories written about the origin of the Freemasons.

Three sons of William Alexander (who had received Nova Scotia from King James I, and who founded the Baronets of Nova Scotia) were among the first seven Freemasons in history. They were William Jr. and Anthony Alexander, being numbers one and two, and Henry Alexander coming along later at number seven.

Of the remainder –

Number three to be initiated was Sir Alexander Strachan of Thornton, who was a Baronet of Nova Scotia and is listed as the third of the first three Freemasons in history, as of July 3, 1634.

Alexander Strachan was also a member of the King's Privy Council, as were Sir Francis Bacon, and William Alexander Sr.

Number four was Sir Archibald Stewart. Of course King James I, who gave Nova Scotia to William Sr., and the king's son, Charles I, who established the Baronets program, were both Stewarts/Stuarts. One Stuart and four Stewarts became Baronets of Nova Scotia.

Number five was David Ramsay, son of Sir Gilbert Ramsay, Baronet of Nova Scotia.

Number six was Alexander Allardyce. Agnes Graham of Stirling married John Alexander, another son of Sir William Alexander. Agnes was the half sister to John Allardyce, the father of Alexander Allardyce. This would make John Alexander an uncle of sorts to Alexander Allardyce, tying Allardyce to the Nova Scotia story.

Allardyce was also a neighbor and friend of Alexander Strachan, one of the first three Freemasons, and one Masonic historians has stated: "The probability is that Mr. Allardyce was introduced to the Lodge by Sir Alexander Strachan, his near neighbor, with whose family, and that of Sir Anthony Alexander, he appears to have had familiar intercourse."

The significance of the first seven Freemasons in history being this closely associated with the Baronets of Nova Scotia cannot be overstated.

Out of thousands of potential "first Freemasons" in Scotland, the first seven have direct connections to the Baronets of Nova Scotia. This has to mean something very important, and as one Masonic historian put it, "The initiation of these non-stonemasons is of major significance for our understanding of the origins and development of modern Freemasonry."

And let us not forget that James Maclean, descendant of a Knights Templar, and of a Baronet of Nova Scotia, was Grand Master of the Freemasons in France, while still a member of the Scottish Freemasons, and still Chief of Clan Maclean, or that one of the earliest owners of the Money Pit lot was also a MacLean descendant.

Not only do these early records of the first Freemasons in history directly connect this organization to the Baronets of Nova Scotia, but they also connect the Freemasons somewhat directly to the Knights Templar.

The clans of Scotland are the very link in how all of these organizations are connected – the Knights Templar, the Baronets of Nova Scotia, and the Freemasons.

This information comes not just from my own decades of research into Scottish history, and my accompanying appointment as a Fellow with the Society of Antiquaries of Scotland, but also from accepted Freemasonry origin stories, from official government documents in Scotland, from the traditions of the very clans involved in these movements, and from a very logical connecting of the dots. Whether Oak Island is involved in this thread of history, or not, the thread is still amazing.

However, I believe Oak Island is involved – and in a big way.

I've already shown how items of value could have been taken to Nova Scotia under the watchful eye of the same clans I spoke about above; how these items were protected from search or seizure due to a special "safe passage" decree written by King Charles I; how the Scots of Port Royal were forced out no later than April 27th, facing a likely spring storm in the North Atlantic (based on scientific weather records); how they could have taken a straight tack to the back of Mahone Bay and found protection in deep waters behind Oak Island (based on a scientific depth scan of these waters) under the watchful eye of their French ally, Claude de la Tour, whose ownership of the lands around Lunenburg is proven by his Baronet charter.

Further, I've shown that many pieces of finished lumber found on Oak Island could fall into a carbon dating window that would include 1632, and some non-biological items found there, which defy carbon dating, are still dated, quite often, to the 1600s.

Finally, I've shown how Nova Scotia received its name and its Coat of Arms at the very same time in history that I am projecting for the burial on Oak Island of some type of valuable items by members of these same Scottish clans.

Sir John Mackenzie was a Baronet of Nova Scotia beginning in 1628, the year the first ship of settlers headed there from Scotland and England. He purchased 16,000 acres along the Gulf of Canada. His son Sir George Mackenzie was the co-founder of the Royal Society of London along with Sir Robert Moray.

Robert Moray is one of the shining stars of early Freemasonry. His initiation, in 1641, was important for a few reasons. He was the first speculative Freemason to be initiated on English soil. Briefly, Moray was part of the Scottish army that occupied, after besieging, Newcastle-upon-Tyne, England, during the so-called "Bishops' Wars" (1639 – 1640).

Members of the Lodge of Edinburgh were pioneers attached to the army to build bridges, fortifications etc. and they held a special meeting to initiate Moray and another army general, Alexander Hamilton. There is nothing unusual in this, as this was a common practice known as "out entries," as attested to by a number of similar initiations noted in various lodge records. It also accords well with Scottish Masonic belief that a lodge is not a place, but rather a gathering of like minded men who come together for the purposes of Freemasonry.

Moray co-founded the Royal Society and became its first president. The society's inaugural meeting was held on Wednesday, November 28, 1660, at Gresham College, London, attended by 12 eminent gentlemen. These 12 prepared a list of 40 other equally eminent gentlemen to be invited to join the new society.

The Royal Society still holds its annual meeting on Saint Andrew's Day (November 30th) in honor of the Scot who was its first president.

In July of 1665, Sir Robert Moray gave a lecture on the use of a charcoal-fired furnace with a 28 to 30 foot high chimney designed to draw fresh air down into a mining shaft. Charcoal was found 30 feet down in the Money Pit, possibly indicating a furnace meant to draw fresh air down to workers digging the pit, making Moray's talk possibly related in some way to the actual building of the Money Pit, through his knowledge gained by association with the Baronets of Nova Scotia.

Moray has an even closer connection to our Nova Scotia story. An alternate spellings for his name was Murray. In fact, his whole family used Murray for many years until his father's sons began using Moray. His father was Sir Mungo Murray, Baronet of Nova Scotia.

Five Murray men were among the original Baronets of Nova Scotia, all signing up within the first few years, from 1625 to 1630. One of these men was William Murray, father of Mungo (who inherited his father's barony), and grandfather of Robert Moray. Robert Moray, the man considered one of the most illustrious of early Freemasons, was the son and grandson of Baronets of Nova Scotia, and co-founded the Royal Society along with George Mackenzie, also the son of a Baronet.

Robert Moray's family came from one of the most heavily populated centers of Knights Templarism, namely County Moray. His younger brother, William Moray, eventually followed in the footsteps of Anthony Alexander and Henry Alexander as Master of Works for Scotland. This powerful position is what led to the first Freemasons in history, as I will soon explain.

But, believe it or not, that isn't all to this story.

You may remember that William Alexander got his start in the power structure of Scotland as the tutor for one Archibald or Gylascop Campbell, the 7th Earl of Argyll. Gylascop's son James was the leader of the Scots Guard, or *Garde Écossaise*, the elite force of Scotsmen who protected the French Royal family.

This organization had deteriorated until George Gordon (husband to a Campbell woman, son of a Stewart woman, and a relative of Robert Gordon who received Cape Breton) decided, in 1632, the very year the Scots left Nova Scotia, that he should revive the Scots Guards. Gylascop's son James was put in charge, and was followed by who else but Robert Moray.

This move put one of the earliest Freemasons, and a son and grandson of Baronets of Nova Scotia, deep within the Royal court of France.

Charles I, as mentioned earlier, was married to the Catholic Princess Henrietta Maria of France, sister to the French king, with whom he made the deal leading to the Port Royal Scots being forced to leave Nova Scotia in 1632. Robert Moray is thought, by many scholars, to have been a spy for Cardinal Richelieu, King Louis XIII's chief minister. It seems his main job was to serve as a intermediary between Louis XIII and Charles I.

Remember, this all happened directly after the Scots were forced out of Nova Scotia, and just as men associated with the Baronets of Nova Scotia were becoming the first Freemasons in history.

All of this very powerful history shows an undeniable link between the Baronets of Nova Scotia and the Freemasons.

The ritual of the Royal Arch is not mentioned in Freemasonry at least until 1744, but more likely around 1750. My theory is that it took that long for the practical, pragmatic story told by the Alexander boys, and other Baronets of Nova Scotia, of the 1632 burial of items in the nine-level Money Pit of Oak Island, to become a "spiritualized" ritual called the Royal Arch Degree.

The following is from a book on the origins of the Freemasons. This excerpt shows that the Royal Arch did not come into vogue until at least the middle of the 1700s. It was NOT some ancient ritual from Egypt, the Middle East, or even from the days of Rosslyn Chapel.

It reads:

The Charter of Constitution, which was then adopted (in the 19th century), proceeds upon the assumption that the "Royal Arch" had existed in Scotland prior to the erection of the Grand Lodge – and that it was embraced in the "Degrees of Freemasons," the jurisdiction of which had from time immemorial been vested in the Barons of Roslin. **This is an erroneous statement.** *The earliest allusion to the Royal Arch*

Degree extant is contained in a work of Dr. D'Assigney, printed at Dublin in 1744, of the existence of which there were doubts until the recent discovery of a copy by Brother William James Hughan, of Truro. The Arch obtained a footing in Scotland about the middle of last century, through the medium of Military Lodges which had themselves become acquainted with the degree in their intercourse with Irish Masons. It is alleged that the Ancient Lodge of Stirling was, in 1743, the first in this country (Scotland) to practise the degree, but of this there is no authentic evidence.

It would be a true bonus if the Lodge of Stirling was the first place the Royal Arch Degree was practiced, as that was the home to the Alexander family.

Another book states: "The Royal Arch Degree seems not to have been known to what are called modern Masons until as late as about 1750."

If in fact the Money Pit was inspired by the Royal Arch ritual, it would have had to have been constructed between about 1750 and its discovery in 1795. It would seem very unlikely that large ships with substantial crews could have anchored off Oak Island and carried out the creation of the Money Pit unnoticed by French settlers living just across Mahone Bay from Oak Island, at Chester, Nova Scotia, at that very time.

Another reason to disbelieve the story of the Royal Arch ritual inspiring the Money Pit is simply that there was no great amount of carbon dated pieces of finished lumber found in the various digs on Oak Island dating from the mid-1700s, but plenty from the mid-1600s.

There is one last stone to turn over in the establishment of the Freemasons, led by the sons of Sir William Alexander, and by Baronets of Nova Scotia.

As we've shown, in 1634, just two years after the return of the Port Royal Scots from Nova Scotia, William Alexander Jr. joined his brother Anthony as the first two Freemasons in history.

While William Jr. was in Nova Scotia, Anthony had been sent to Europe, by King Charles I, to study classic architecture.

Back on December 21, 1583, James VI appointed William Schaw as principal "Maister o' Wark" (Master of Works) to the Crown of Scotland for life, with responsibility for all royal castles and palaces. Schaw saw the need for the stonemason lodges of Scotland to become more highly organized and governed.

These lodges, in the simplest of terms, were often temporary lodging built for stonemasons who were working on long-term projects in a certain area. Unlike many craftsmen, their job called for a lot of travel.

Schaw issued some standards for these stonemason guilds, and also recognized the Sinclair family of Rosslyn Chapel as the traditional patron and protector of the craft of stonemasonry across Scotland.

Schaw was followed first by Sir David Cunningham, who was a relative of the king, then by James Murray, a forefather of Robert Moray, who was then followed by Walter Murray, another relative of Robert Moray.

Each of these men had practical skill in the building trade and were easily accepted as the Master of Works overseeing projects that the stonemason guilds would be working on, especially royal or religious buildings.

However, when Anthony Alexander's name was put forth as the heir to Walter Murray's position as Master of Works, William Sinclair (a descendant of both William Sinclair, who built Rosslyn Chapel, and of Henry Sinclair, who is said to have made a trip to Nova Scotia in 1398) objected on the grounds that the Sinclairs were the long-time patrons of the stonemasons and that he should have a chance at becoming Master of Works, not someone like Anthony Alexander, who had no real day-to-day experience in building and/or maintaining elaborate structures like cathedrals and royal palaces.

Sinclair put all his political allies to work to stop Anthony. Meanwhile, William Alexander Sr. did the same, in order to get this coveted position for his son.

One of the main objections was that Anthony belonged to no builder's guild and so his father arranged for him to be initiated into the stonemasons' guild at Edinburgh. For whatever reason, he was joined by his bother William Jr. and Sir Alexander Strachan, both with ties to the Baronets of Nova Scotia. Once the door was opened, Baronet-related initiates flooded in, with the first seven Freemasons having absolute connections to the Scots adventure in Nova Scotia, and the most illustrious of early Freemasons, Robert Moray, also having a father and grandfather who were Baronets of Nova Scotia.

As mentioned earlier, Moray, a son of a Baronet of Nova Scotia, co-founded the Royal Society of Edinburgh with another son of a Baronet, George Mackenzie.

The connections of Freemasonry to Oak Island are legendary. Although my theory suggests the Money Pit was first created out of convenience or necessity by the evacuating Scots of Port Royal, in 1632, it is entirely possible that once so many early Freemasons associated with the Baronets of Nova Scotia could get arrangements made, they may have returned to search for the pit, in order to recover what was buried there.

Again, Mark Finnan has written extensively on the involvement of Freemasons, throughout the years, in the dig at the Money Pit. In one of his books he specifically states: "...it is almost a certainty that organizers of the first coordinated dig ...were Masonicly associated."

He further states, "Successive treasure hunts throughout the past two hundred years often involve men who were prominent members of Masonic lodges. Some had passed through the higher levels of initiation, and a few even held high the highest offices possible within the Fraternity."

I'll leave it to others to tell, in detail, of the Masonic connections to the various digs on Oak Island, and to all the Masonic symbology found there.

But just a few examples include these men:

A. O. Creighton was the treasurer of the Oak Island Association, 1861-1866. He was a Freemason, as was Jotham McCully, the corporate secretary.

Frederick Blair, whose family explored Oak Island as far back as 1863, was a prominent member of the lodge at Amherst, Nova Scotia, and treasure hunter William Chappel was an active Freemason; his son Mel served as Provincial Grand Master for Nova Scotia from 1944 through 1946.

Gilbert Hedden, who carried out a search from 1934 to 1938, and Edwin Hamilton, who followed Hedden, were both Freemasons.

While there were plenty of others, perhaps the most famous person to be involved at Oak Island was Franklin D. Roosevelt, who was also a Freemason.

Even two famous investors in Oak Island that were also Hollywood movie stars, were associated with Freemasonry. John Wayne was a Freemason, like his father before him, receiving his craft degrees on July 11, 1970, at the Marion McDaniel Lodge 56, Tucson, Arizona. In December of that year, he joined the York Rite Bodies in California and became a Shriner in the Al Malaikah Shrine Temple, located in Long Beach.

Errol Flynn is the other actor who is associated with Oak Island as an investor. He is said to have been a Freemason, although information on this seems scarce.

My point is that, if the Freemasons have been extraordinarily interested in the Money Pit and Oak Island, through the years, it may not be due to the fact that they originally created it as an actual buried treasure vault, a teaching tool, or as a practical joke (as some have suggested), but rather because pragmatic information on how to retrieve the buried items was imparted to the Freemasons through the very first non-operative, speculative Freemasons in history.

The first seven Freemasons in history included men associated directly with the Baronets of Nova Scotia, not to mention the most famous early Freemason, Sir Robert Moray, who was also connected to the Baronets of Nova Scotia, through his father and grandfather.

Again, these historic facts cannot be ignored or left out of the questions about Oak Island. As one writer put it, in speaking about Freemasons, "Theirs is not, they insist, a 'secret society' but a 'society with secrets.'"

I believe one of these secrets included information on the burial of items on Oak Island, in 1632, by Scots from Port Royal, who were being ousted from Nova Scotia; that men associated with this colony became several of the first Freemasons and buried this secret in that organization until such time as a recovery of these items could be undertaken; that the pragmatic information surrounding the burial pit became veiled in the allegory of the Royal Arch Degree; and that, once the Money Pit was discovered in 1795, this hidden knowledge floated back to the surface as Freemasons eagerly joined in on the search for treasure on Oak Island.

This theory has none of the mysticism that often accompanies Oak Island theories, but rather is based on historic, scientific, pragmatic information, and on logical conclusions drawn from this information.

Therefore, it is, at least in this way, very different from the typical tale told of this mystery.

Another question that often arises is – Why didn't the men who buried the items at Oak Island return to retrieve them? I will answer that question next, using the same type of historic, scientific, pragmatic information, and logical conclusions.

It should be said that there is some evidence of Alexander family members living in Nova Scotia after the 1632 evacuation. These may have included Claude de la Tour's wife, who was related to the Alexanders, William Alexander Jr., who may have returned and died in Nova Scotia, and William Jr.'s brother, John, whose own son John raised a family at New Ross.

In fact, on May 11, 1633, almost exactly one year after the Port Royal evacuation, Sir William Alexander received a royal patent "for the sole trade in all and singular the regions, countreys, dominions, and all places whatsoever adjacent to the River and Gulf of Canada, and the sole traffick from thence and the places adjoyning, for beaver skins and wool, and all other skins from wild beasts, for 31 yeares."

The Scottish Parliament ratified all of Sir William's rights on June 28, 1633, including – "all liberties, priviledges, honnours, juristictions, and dignities respective, therein mentioned."

This included his dominion over Nova Scotia and his leadership of the Baronets of Nova Scotia. Baronet titles were sold until 1638, which included land grants, though these grants may have never been claimed.

It may be that some of the Alexanders did in fact return to retrieve or at least protect what was left behind, at a time when their family in Scotland was experiencing many unusual deaths, while simultaneously advancing in government and social circles. Others may have stayed in Nova Scotia much longer than first thought.

Chapter Eight
'TIL DEATH DO US PART

It has not been unusual to see groups of Freemasons visit Oak Island in any given recent year. Their attraction to this island is still strong and, as we've seen, many Freemasons have been involved in the digs there.

Whether my theory is correct in that the Money Pit foreshadowed the Royal Arch Degree, or the more common theory that the Money Pit was patterned after the Royal Arch Degree, the question remains – Why did it take so long for Freemasons, or anyone for that matter, to return to Oak Island to retrieve the treasure?

The answer is simple – they all died!

Anthony Alexander, son of the founder of the Baronets of Nova Scotia, and a man who battled politically with William Sinclair (the traditional head of the stonemason guilds) for the position of Master of Works, from 1630 onward, is listed as the second of the first three Freemasons in history, as of July 3, 1634.

Anthony was dead three years later, by 1637, at the young age of 47, and just three days after his final confirmation as Master of Works! He joined the Freemasons along with his brother, William Jr., the actual leader of the Scots in Nova Scotia, who is listed as the first of three Freemasons in history, in 1634.

In 1630, Anthony was appointed as the co-Master of Works along with James Murray, son of the previous Master of Works. Murray died in December of 1634, leaving Anthony as sole Master of Works.

Sinclair made one appeal after another to King Charles I, and according to Anthony, Sinclair had "by some sinister information" prevented the king's seal from actually being applied to Anthony's appointment letter as Master of Works.

Sinclair tried to use his political influence to stop Anthony. Finally, in a letter to Sinclair, written in 1637, the king said that he would be willing to consider Sinclair as leader of the masons and builders as long as it didn't interfere with Anthony Alexander being Master of Works. Three days later Anthony was dead!

Anthony was married to the daughter of Sir Henry Wardlaw, a Baronet of Nova Scotia who owned 16,000 acres there called the Barony of Wardlaw. Sir Henry also died in 1637, the same year as his son-in-law!

For whatever reason, William Alexander Jr. was listed as the first Freemason, even though it seems that it was Anthony's appointment as Master of Works that led to the brothers joining as the first non-operative Masons.

William died the year after Anthony, in 1638, and was only 34-years-old. William possibly died while in Nova Scotia. More on this soon. That same year, 1638, another Alexander brother (Robert) died at age 25.

Instead of then choosing William Sinclair to become Master of Works, Charles I favored another Alexander brother, Henry. Henry Alexander, also a son of the founder of the Baronets, joined as the seventh Freemason in history, in 1638, and inherited Anthony's title of Master of Works for Scotland. He died young at age 42, in 1647 (although some say as early as 1645, at age 40).

The window of Alexander-related deaths spanned 1636 to 1647, an eleven year period, at a time when any attempt to return to Nova Scotia would likely have been thought about, if not actually undertaken.

Meanwhile, William Alexander Sr.'s fortunes were fading fast. In addition to the money he personally lost on the Nova Scotia adventure, other Baronets were pressuring him and King Charles I to either revive the Baronets program or return some of their money.

It seemed that no matter what Sir William tried there was no reversing his fate, and he died heavily in debt. It is said that his debtors surrounded his deathbed, giving him no peace right up until his passing in 1640.

William Jr.'s only son, William III, also died in 1640, at an extremely young age, after being named Lord Stirling, upon the death of the father of all these men – Sir William Alexander Sr., Privy Council member, Secretary of State, and founder of the Baronets of Nova Scotia.

Another brother, John Alexander, was married to Agnes Graham. She died young, in 1636, and John died in 1642, at age 30. He also had ties to Nova Scotia.

On April 20, 1635, John Alexander was, conjointly with his father, appointed Master of Minerals and Metals in Scotland (*Reg. Mag. Sig., vol. iv., p. 60, Paper Register*).

He was afterwards nominated General of the Mint, and served until 1641, shortly before his death.

Meanwhile, the Alexander's French ally, Claude de la Tour, died in or just after 1636, in Nova Scotia. Remember, he was married to an Alexander-related wife. And then we have Sir George Home, Baronet of Nova Scotia, and leader of the Port Royal Scots, while William Jr. was away. He died in or around 1636, as well. He was likely still in Nova Scotia at the time, based on a lack of records in Scotland, after he left for Nova Scotia.

Here you have at least eleven people in eleven years, all tied in some manner to the Nova Scotia adventure, passing away, including a father, a father-in-law, five sons, a daughter-in-law, a grandson, and two allies on a completely different continent. Two more brothers died at ages 52 and 55. All of these people were as close to the Baronets of Nova Scotia program, and any connection to Oak Island it might have had, as anyone could get.

Charles I, who chartered the Baronets, was beheaded by Oliver Cromwell's troops in 1649, and within two years, David Alexander, whose privateering ships were to accompany the Baronets settlers to Nova Scotia in 1628, was captured by Cromwell's forces (in 1651).

David had at one time been considered, or possibly even appointed as Master of Works. Both Anthony and Henry definitely held that coveted position.

Who or what was responsible for the deaths of all these people?

In the end, nine Alexander males, ranging in ages from an infant, to 25, 30, 34, 42, 47, 52, 55 and 73 years of age, were dead. Anthony died just three days after King Charles confirmed him in the position of Master of

Works for Scotland, after a long-fought political battle with William Sinclair over this position.

It does seem that Anthony's death must have been completely unexpected as the king had just fought a long and hard political battle with William Sinclair to see Anthony appointed as Master of Works.

That this family had enemies is proven by their troubles with William Sinclair and Oliver Cromwell, each representing a different side of the political/religious split. The Alexander's were in a squeeze play, it appears. All the while, whatever they knew about anything left behind in Nova Scotia could not be acted upon openly for lack of money, constant deaths in the family, and an ever-increasing enemies list.

Sinclair may have been doubly aggravated in that, instead of choosing him to become Master of Works, on the death of Anthony Alexander, King Charles chose another Alexander brother, Henry, who actually had no architectural training.

So here's a list of suspects not meant to incriminate anyone in particular, but just to help solve the riddle:

Suspect No. 1) Oliver Cromwell – Civil war had broken out first in Scotland, then spread to Ireland, and finally to England. In March 1625, Charles I became king. When his first Parliament met in June, trouble immediately arose because of the general distrust of one of Charles' closest aides, the Duke of Buckingham.

The Puritans predominated in the House of Commons, whereas the sympathies of the king were with what came to be known as the High Church Party, which stressed the value of the prayer book and the maintenance of ritual. The term originated in and has been principally associated with the Anglican/Episcopal religion, where it describes Anglican churches using a number of ritual practices associated in the popular mind with Roman Catholicism.

Charles was even thought to be a secret Catholic, and had married a Catholic bride. Thus antagonism soon arose between the new king and the House of Commons, and Parliament refused to vote him the right to levy customs duties except on conditions that would increase their powers, even though this right had been granted to previous monarchs for life.

The second Parliament of the reign, meeting in February 1626, proved to be even more critical of the king's government.

The failure of a naval expedition against the Spanish, in the previous autumn, was blamed on Charles' aide, the Duke of Buckingham, and for this the House of Commons tried to impeach him for treason. To prevent this, Charles dissolved Parliament in June of 1626.

During the major planning of the Baronets of Nova Scotia program, and in desperate need of funds, the king imposed a forced loan, which his judges declared illegal. He dismissed the chief justice and ordered the arrest of more than 70 knights and gentlemen who refused to contribute. His high-handed actions added to the sense of grievance that was widely discussed in the next Parliament.

By the time Charles's third Parliament met (March 1628), Buckingham's expedition to aid the French Protestants at La Rochelle had been decisively repelled and the king's government was thoroughly discredited.

Some may remember that it was from the port of La Rochelle, France, that the Knights Templar ships were said to have set sail in 1307, just on the eve of their dissolution by the French king. Whether this was a factor in Buckingham's interest in La Rochelle is not yet known.

From here things began to settle down a little, with Buckingham having been assassinated and King Charles bending slightly to the will of Parliament.

On the whole, the kingdom seems to have enjoyed some degree of prosperity until 1639, when Charles became involved in a war against the Scots.

One of the most intense enemies of Charles I was Oliver Cromwell. He became a Puritan after undergoing a religious conversion in the 1630s, taking a generally tolerant view towards the many Protestant sects of this period.

Cromwell was elected a Member of Parliament for Huntingdon in 1628, and for Cambridge in the Short (1640) and Long (1640–1649) Parliaments.

He entered the English Civil War on the side of the "Roundheads" or Parliamentarians. Nicknamed "Old Ironsides," he demonstrated his ability as a commander and was quickly promoted from leading a single cavalry troop to being one of the principal commanders, playing an important role in the defeat of the royalist forces.

Cromwell was one of the signers of King Charles I's death warrant in 1649, and he dominated the short-lived Commonwealth of England again as a member of Parliament (1649–1653).

He was selected to take command of the English campaign in Ireland in 1649–1650. Cromwell's forces defeated the Confederate and Royalist coalition in Ireland and occupied the country, bringing an end to the Irish Confederate Wars. During this period, a series of penal laws were passed against Roman Catholics (a significant minority in England and Scotland, but the vast majority in Ireland), and a substantial amount of their land was confiscated. Cromwell also led a campaign against the Scottish army between 1650 and 1651.

In 1654, Cromwell acknowledged Charles de la Tour's inheritance of Nova Scotia from his father, Claude de la Tour. Charles de la Tour immediately sold his rights to two Englishmen for enough money to pay off his debts.

Cromwell didn't do this out of the kindness of his heart. He wanted non-debatable control over Nova Scotia.

Since Cromwell's interest was so high in Nova Scotia, and his Puritan leanings were in direct conflict with supporters of Charles I, he may well have been behind the deaths of Sir William Alexander and his sons and family members.

Cromwell was responsible for Charles I's beheading, his troops did capture David Alexander, and he did make a deal for Nova Scotia with Charles de la Tour, so there is plenty of proof of his interest and involvement.

Suspect No. 2) William Sinclair – Let me count the ways Sinclair was involved in this whole Nova Scotia adventure. To begin with, it was his own ancestor who was said to have made the first attempt at creating a New Scotland in Nova Scotia. The jury is still out on this, although many people believe it, and I provide a fair amount of evidence for this legend in my earlier book *Oak Island Missing Links*.

Next, we know the Sinclairs were involved with both the Knights Templar and with the stonemason lodges of Scotland. William was extremely upset with the fact that Anthony Alexander, and later Henry Alexander, were appointed to a position of Master of Works, a position that he felt he deserved, due to this involvement.

At this time in history it was not uncommon for many people to settle their scores through the murder of their enemy. There is no evidence that Sinclair did so in this instance, but he certainly had the motive and plenty of opportunity, since his own friends within the stonemason lodges were, no doubt, keeping him abreast of the activities of the first Freemasons, three of whom were sons of William Alexander, and all of whom died at very young ages.

It could be that he felt this new type of non-operative, speculative version of Freemasonry was an affront to all the true stonemasons throughout Scotland for whom he served as protector and patron.

Suspect No.3) Masons – If word was spread around about a treasure buried on Oak Island, along with directions on how to dig down through the nine-levels of the Money Pit, a secret group of stonemasons may have quietly eliminated the competition for the treasure. Certainly, men have killed others for next to nothing throughout history, and if the Oak Island treasure was as grand as some have said, it would certainly present a motive for unscrupulous, often poor operative masons to take advantage of. It may have been a rogue group of masons, not the Freemason fraternity itself, who were waiting for their own chance to recover the treasure.

Suspect No. 4) Others involved in the Money Pit burial – There is a possibility that upwards of 200 people were forced to evacuate Port Royal in 1632. We know 40 lived through the first winter. But several other trips were made there by William Alexander Jr., over the next few years, and so the true number living at Port Royal in 1632 is not known. It should be noted that the French needed a force of 300 soldiers to evacuate the Scots.

Anyone with intimate knowledge of the Money Pit burial could have conspired with others to eliminate competition for the recovery of what might be buried on Oak Island.

Suspect No. 5) Others who wanted the secret kept – If, in fact, rare or vary valuable items were secreted away on Oak Island, there may have been a faction of Scottish noblemen, scholars, or antiquarians who wanted these things to remain buried forever. If that was the plan, so far it has worked quite well.

Regardless of who might be the culprit, it is nearly impossible to believe that eleven significant people, with important connections to the Baronets of Nova Scotia, simply died of natural causes or disease over an eleven year period, with two more sons following close behind, also at young ages. Anthony's death had to be unexpected simply because of the huge battle fought to get him appointed as Master of Works, a battle won just three days before he died. Something extraordinary was happening for all these people to die in such a short time, and at such young ages.

It also has to be kept in mind that this era in Scottish history was filled with superstitious beliefs that may have somehow played a role in the demise of the Alexander clan.

Witch hunts "officially" began in Scotland in 1620, although as early as 1616 those with second sight were being accused of being witches. Studies of second sight in the Highlands would soon be undertaken, beginning with *The Secret Commonwealth*, first issued in 1691, by Rev. Robert Kirk. In this book, Kirk states that he had found five curiosities in Scotland – brownies (little people), second sight, the Mason Word, charms, and the ability to be bullet-proof.

So, it can be seen that the Mason Word was already relegated to the mystical realm.

The earliest known reference to the Mason Word is in a poem written in 1630, which states "We have the Mason Word and second sight, things for to come we can foretell alright."

The Mason Word began pragmatically as a way to identify true craftsmen at a time when stonemasons would be called to work on projects in diverse areas of Scotland, and would need to set up a temporary shelter on site, which became known as a lodge.

This was all practical, as many of these masons were just getting by financially, and so a brotherhood or guild was developed for self-protection. It was natural, at a time when religion played such a central role in society, and was being torn asunder through the various factions of Catholic, and a variety of Protestant religious/political pressures, that these lodges would take on some spiritual fellowship aspects.

What began as a secret word, secret handshake, and even a secret stance, which would allow one qualified mason to recognize another, simply dissolved into something equated with second sight, which in itself may just be, in many cases, what we might call "street smarts" or "life experience," which allows for an imaginative and educated guess.

Throughout history, humankind has used symbols to represent ideas. The earliest Scots were called Picts because they tattooed their bodies with symbols. Celtic art is nothing if not symbols.

Clans had their flags and tartans signifying that they belonged to one group, and they even had a sprig of some type, like heather, in their hats to identify each other while in the middle of a fierce battle.

These were all pragmatic devices that spoke volumes with no words actually being uttered.

In fact, it can be said that humankind always used images and symbols to impart ideas, from cave drawings to Chinese calligraphy, to Egyptian hieroglyphics, and even to the English alphabet. So it wouldn't be unique for Freemasons to use symbols or symbology to represent a pragmatic idea or important information.

Throughout history mankind has often managed to turn the pragmatic into the mystical. Astrology, for example, was once just an aspect of a very pragmatic astronomy attempting to understand the movement of the stars in order to predict when to plant crops, or how to navigate. Now it is usually relegated to a newspaper column or simplified book on which some people actually base life decisions, or at least find guidance in.

The "pragmatic" is often tagged with the label of being mystical or ceremonial, or ritual, and I believe this might have happened when William Alexander Jr., along with his brother Anthony, and another Baronet of Nova Scotia, as the first three non-operative, speculative Freemasons in history, imparted the knowledge of the nine levels of the Money Pit, meant as a road map to recovering what was buried there, to fellow Freemasons they may have felt they could trust. Through the years, this misunderstood knowledge may actually have inspired the nine levels ritual of the Royal Arch Degree.

Meanwhile, the nine-level Money Pit on Oak Island lay undisturbed until it was stumbled upon by young men out looking for pirate treasure. The rest is history, or at least mystery, and through the years the mysteries just kept piling up, as serious folks were drilling down.

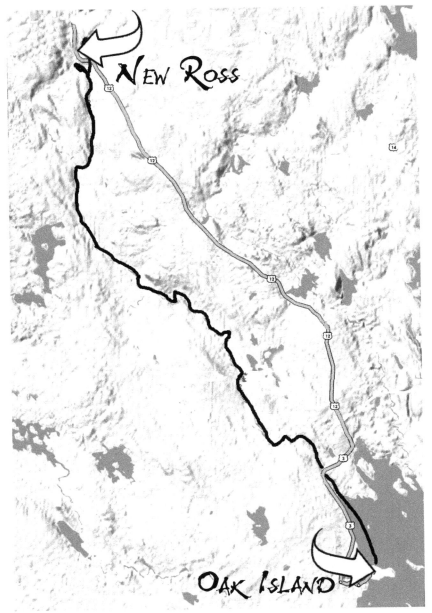

The distance from the New Ross area to Oak Island is about 20 miles.
The solid line shows Gold River from New Ross to Oak Island.
The gray line shows the modern highway from New Ross to Oak Island.

Chapter Nine

NEW ROSS

In the last chapter, I told you that everyone associated with the Baronets of Nova Scotia program had died.

But that's not completely true.

In the April 1903 issue of a magazine called *The William and Mary Quarterly* an article appeared, written by B.R. Wellford, entitled "The Alexander Family in England."

In it, the author states, "The eldest son, William, Viscount Canada, being his majesty's resident in Nova Scotia, died there in his father's lifetime."

Could William Jr. have returned to Nova Scotia to further the aims of the Baronets, or of the Alexander family? It looks like that could be the case.

Another point of interest is that William Jr. had a son by a Mi'kmaq woman, almost certainly the daughter of Segipt, the chief chosen to represent the Mi'kmaq in an overseas visit to meet the English king. It was very common for a white leader in early North American history to marry the wife of the local Indian chief.

Regardless of the genealogy of William Jr.'s Mi'kmaq wife, from this union comes a branch of the family of LaBlanc in Nova Scotia. This is attested to (to their highest degree of probability) by Family Tree DNA.

I consider Family Tree DNA to be the best DNA testing group in the business, having worked with them for over 15 years.

Now, William Alexander, Jr. would have an even stronger reason to want to see the Scots settlement in Nova Scotia succeed, since he had a son living there by the name of Daniel LeBlanc.

It is said that this son was surnamed LeBlanc by his mother, because his skin was so light in color. The name Daniel is said to come from the first name of the ship's captain that took Chief Segipt to England, and LeBlanc translates as "white" in English.

For whatever reason, the mother did not name the child with the surname of Alexander. Perhaps William Jr. didn't want her to. Regardless, Family Tree DNA gives the highest probability rating that Daniel LeBlanc was the son of William Alexander, Jr.

This son of William, Jr. did not die young, as the LeBlanc family continued in Nova Scotia, and has expanded, as most families do, only recently discovering their link to the Alexander surname (from back in the 17th century) through DNA research. The son of William Jr., who died in 1640, in England, had to be by another woman, presumably William's British wife.

With a son and perhaps a wife in Nova Scotia, with a lot of money and pride invested in Port Royal, and with perhaps secret knowledge of the burial of items on Oak Island, it is not out of the question that William returned to Nova Scotia, and, as the magazine article mentioned above states, he may well have died there.

William Jr. was not the only Alexander in Nova Scotia after the ousting of the Port Royal Scots. We already know that his relative had married Claude de la Tour, who owned the coastline 30 to 40 miles inland from Yarmouth to Lunenburg, and that she turned down a trip back to Great Britain to stay in Nova Scotia with her French husband.

But there may have been another Alexander branch in nearby New Ross – that of William Jr.'s brother John.

Of course, New Ross wasn't named as such back in the early 1600s, as far as we know. It is said to be named after a place in Ireland called New Ross. Obviously, to be "new," the Irish New Ross had to be named after an old Ross, and the old Ross is in Scotland. In fact, the region of Ross has always encompassed a large part of the Scottish Highlands. The 12th Chief of Clan Ross led 1,000 of his clansmen against Oliver Cromwell at the Battle of Worcester in 1651. However, many were captured and transported to the colonies in North America, perhaps bringing the Ross name with them.

Ross is still one of the five most frequent surnames to be found in the northern Highlands, and the 16th most frequently registered in the whole of Scotland.

It would be entirely appropriate that a place in New Scotland would be named New Ross, regardless of the many origin stories related to this New Ross name.

Two things we do know about New Ross are:

1) That it is located towards the headwaters of Gold River, which runs into Mahone Bay, just above Oak Island, and...

2) Alexander Alexander is said, in Alexander family records, to have been born at New Ross, in 1650. He was the son of John Alexander, and the grandson son of John Alexander, co-Master of Minerals and Metals for Great Britain, and the great-grandson of William Alexander Sr., the other co-Master of Minerals and Metals (and the man behind the Baronets of Nova Scotia).

An Ancestry.com posting on the Alexander family genealogy claims that William Jr. lived in Nova Scotia for 12 years. If he died in 1638, then he must have first gone to Nova Scotia in 1626. This would not be out of the question, since it is known his father sent ships there in 1622 and 1623. Plus, William Jr. is known to have made many trips back and forth, and so he could have easily been in Nova Scotia in 1626, in a land his father had owned for five years, at that point.

John, son of John, grandson of William Sr., is also said to have been born in Nova Scotia in 1625. He seems to have stayed right along, since it was his son Alexander who was supposed to have been born at New Ross in 1650. This means William Sr.'s son John must have been in Nova Scotia in 1625, too. At some point, the younger John left Nova Scotia with his son Alexander, and died in Colonial America in 1677. The fact that the Alexanders did not readily give up on Nova Scotia is proven by the fact that the Baronet titles were still being sold as late as 1638, with a land grant included. The titles continued to be sold, without a land grant, up until 1706.

In 1684, 148 Scots settlers arrived in Nova Scotia to rebuild the settlement at Port Royal, showing there was still interest. This new Scots settlement, at the old Port Royal location, was named by the Scots as Stuarts Town, although it was short-lived, and the area is now known as Annapolis Royal.

The point is, the efforts of the Scots to settle Nova Scotia did not end as the Scots left Port Royal in 1632.

Perhaps the efforts of the Alexander family didn't end then, either. One reason may have been gold and silver, as mentioned in the order to leave Port Royal, in 1632.

Also, in William Alexander Sr.'s charter for Nova Scotia, in the same section that named that country with this specific name, it once again states:

Which lands aforesaid, in all time to come, shall enjoy the name of Nova Scotia, in America, which also the aforesaid Sir William shall divide into parts and portions, as to him may seem meet, and give names to the same, according to his pleasure; **together with all mines, as well royal of gold and silver, as other mines of iron, lead, copper, brass, tin, and other minerals whatsoever, with power of digging them, and causing them to be dug out of the earth, of purifying and refining the same, and converting and using them to his own proper use, or to other uses whatsoever, as to the said Sir William Alexander, his heirs or assigns, or those whom it shall have happened that he shall have established in his stead, in the said lands, shall seem meet – reserving only for us and our successors the tenth part of the metal commonly called ore of gold and silver, which hereafter shall be dug up or gained.**

William Alexander divide Nova Scotia into two parts, one called Alexandria and the other called Caledonia. Today, there are five villages and one port still called Caledonia, in Nova Scotia.

New Ross is located only about 20 miles from Oak Island, and about 35 miles or so from Lunenburg.

Why does this matter?

Claude de la Tour, spouse to an Alexander-related woman who stayed in Nova Scotia, was given a charter which included the land 30 to 40 miles inland from Yarmouth to Lunenburg, which would have been at least close to including New Ross. What else is wonderful to know is that, according to a book from the North of England Institute of Mining and Mechanical Engineers, called *Transactions (Vol. XXXI)*, from 1881-82:

The gold fields of Nova Scotia occupy a district extending along the Atlantic Coast from Cape Canso to Yarmouth, and varying in width from ten to forty miles. In the Lunenburg district, and many of the inland valleys there is good farming land, but generally speaking, the district is valued only for its timber and gold mines.

(The book further states:)

The existence of gold in Nova Scotia was conjectured perhaps when Queen Elizabeth, in 1578, in a patent granted to Sir Humphrey Gilbert, made a reservation of one-fifth of all gold and silver he might discover. Later, in a patent issued by Charles I to Sir William Alexander, in 1621, one-tenth of the precious metal was reserved. The names of Bras D'or, Jeu D'or, etc. would seem to show that gold was not unknown among the early French settlers, and it appears on good authority that one hundred and fifty years ago, they washed from the sands of the River Avon, near Windsor, small quantities of gold.

Windsor is also only about 40 miles from Oak Island, the point being that here we have a serious reference to gold being found in or near the area controlled by the Alexander family ally, Claude de la Tour, and a short distance from Gold River, New Ross, and Oak Island.

In another book, *The Gold Fields of Nova Scotia: A Prospectors Handbook*, written in 1915, by Walter H. Prest, of Bedford, Nova Scotia, we read:

The discovery of gold in Nova Scotia is an old, old story, as early documents and geographical names indicate. We have the old names, Cap D'or and Bras D'or, of the early French discoverers. In 1759. the journal of the Rev. John Seacombe of Lunenburg contains references to Gold River.

So, we now know that Gold River was named as such at least by 1759. The author also states:

The gneisses and schists of Shelburne and Yarmouth counties, though entered on the maps as a part of the gold bearing- series, have not so far been proved to contain gold bearing leads of value. A few sights of gold have been reported from Shelburne county but the reports have not been verified. A few sights have also been reported from the gneisses of New Ross.

In laymen's terms, both schists and gneisses are types of metamorphic rocks. They are composed of quartz and feldspar minerals, plus other assorted minerals unique to each type, as well as garnet crystals which sometimes grow within the finer-grained rock.

He goes on to say:

Other mineral bearing faults contain silver bearing galena, one of which, north of Musquodoboit Harbor, show the possibilities of this class of fissures. Discoveries of silver bearing galena in the drift near or on the various granite tracts indicate the existence of other probably valuable deposits.

Finally, this author tells us:

Among the various minerals found in our gold bearing veins are lead, copper, nickel, antimony, cobalt, zinc, iron, silver, arsenic and probably bismuth. They are usually combined in the various ores known as galena, copper pyrites, niccolite or millerite, stibnite, cobaltite or smaltite, zinc blende, iron pyrites, marcasite, mispickel, pyrrhotite, etc. So far they have been of no commercial value. Our granites and gneisses, having been proved to contain tin. A prospector's time may be well repaid by a more extended search than has heretofore been made. A large tract of these rocks occupies the interior of Shelburne, Yarmouth, Digby and Annapolis Counties, and have been but slightly explored.

William Alexander was given the rights to all "gold and silver, as other mines of iron, lead, copper, brass, tin, and other minerals" – most of these being mentioned in the above quote. Also, he had already been heavily involved in mining operations in Scotland before ever setting out on this new adventure to Nova Scotia.

What we've learned in this chapter is that gold and silver were mentioned many times – in the evacuation order of Port Royal, in the original charter of Nova Scotia to William Alexander, in the commission given to Sir Humphrey Gilbert, and in various books on mining in Nova Scotia – with a good share of it lying relatively close to Oak Island, and within the reaches of the charter of Claude de la Tour, an Alexander family ally.

Claude's son Charles, in 1654, accepted an inheritance of his father's Baronet title and land grant from Oliver Cromwell, then immediately sold it to two Englishmen for enough money to pay off his debts.

Somewhere between 1654 and 1659 is when the family of John Alexander left the New Ross, Nova Scotia, area for the American colonies, although some of his descendants appear to have moved to Ireland, or back to Scotland. In the last few decades during which I have been researching and writing on Scottish history, I have learned – and it has been confirmed by other historians – that family traditions are very often found to be true in general, if not always in the fine details.

There is no reason not to believe the Alexander family tradition that William Jr. died in Nova Scotia, that his brother John Alexander had a son, also named John, born in Nova Scotia, in 1625, who then had a son named Alexander, born in 1650, in the area that became New Ross, and who came to America with his father.

Again, it is likely that this younger John left Nova Scotia around 1654-59, after Charles de la Tour sold his father's land to two Englishmen.

What the years 1621 and 1654 have in common is that they fall well within the carbon dating window that I discovered for finished lumber found in Oak Island digs – a window that seems to extend from 1620 to 1660.

It is almost a certainty, at least in my mind, that whatever happened on Oak Island happened during this period, and we know that the allies, Claude de la Tour and the Alexander family, had a vested interest in this area during this period, perhaps even including the mining of gold, silver, and other valuable minerals.

Still, 1632 stands out as the year that holds the best promise for a small fleet of ships taking refuge near Oak Island, out of pragmatic necessity, and, also out of necessity leaving behind something of value buried in the Money Pit. Why else would Oak Island be chosen from among 364 other potential Mahone Bay islands as the site that has held so many artifacts and legends?

This isn't to say that items could not have been buried on other islands, or even on the mainland, but it has been Oak Island that has sparked everyone's imagination, and which has drawn the specific interest of Freemasons.

The Alexander family, and their 1629-32 settlement, stands out as one of the best links of Nova Scotia to Scotland, of New Ross to Oak Island, of Knights Templar families to the Baronets of Nova Scotia, of the Baronets of Nova Scotia to the Freemasons, and of the nine-level Money Pit to the nine-level Royal Arch Degree.

It is all there, in books which show all these deep connections, and which were written long before any modern-day conspiracy theories could have developed.

My theory is simply that valuable items were buried in the Money Pit due to an unexpected arrival of Scots during a storm, in the year 1632. I believe one of the ships sank in what then became the so-called swamp. I think that during one of the early treasure hunts the important items collapsed into natural water tunnels that run under Oak Island, and that a debris field was created based on the direction of the water flow in these tunnels.

I believe that the nine levels were created, with perhaps lesser treasure placed on upper levels to hide the fact that the true treasures were buried further below.

I believe that a charcoal-fired furnace provided the fresh air to those digging at the lower levels, as described by Sir Robert Moray, one of the earliest Freemasons and a son and grandson of Baronets of Nova Scotia.

I believe that information on how the pit was originally constructed was imparted to the earliest of Freemasons, through the Baronets of Nova Scotia, where it lingered (becoming represented by the Royal Arch Degree) until the Money Pit was re-discovered in 1795. I believe Freemasons "in the know" took notice of this discovery and joined in the search as investors and supervisors.

And what better people to be responsible for a sophisticated structure being built on Oak Island than the Alexander family, with three Alexander's – Anthony, Henry, and David – being named Master of Works for Scotland, plus William Alexander Sr. and his son John being named co-Masters of Mining for Scotland?

It's all there – the skill, the means, the motive, and the opportunity!

1398
Sinclair
Voyage

1795
Money Pit
Discovered

1621
Nova Scotia
Charter

1804
Major Digs
At Money Pit
Begin

1632
Scots Leave
Port Royal

2007
Current
Oak Island
Partnership
Begins Its Search

2017
This Author Visits
Oak Island And Writes

*Oak Island
Missing Links*
And
Oak Island 1632

Chapter Ten
In A Nutshell

I am well aware of all the details that have been accumulated as I have been carrying out research for both of my books *Oak Island Missing Links* and *Oak Island 1632*. For every item that has made it into these books, at least one was left behind.

I've always been amazed at just how much information is "out there" in old manuscripts, official government documents, and in my case, old Scottish clan traditions.

While I've done my best to weave these two tapestries, which reveal my version of the mysteries of Oak Island, I know that it can be overwhelming to read about so many occurrences taking place in so many years.

So, I thought for this last chapter that I would create a timeline of significant dates accompanied by a quick paragraph relating why they are significant.

The detail lies not so much in these paragraphs as in the pages of my books, but at least, for those who react well to timelines and visuals, perhaps this will help with the understanding of a history that literally has been continuous from around 1398, with the supposed voyage of Sir Henry Sinclair, to the present day explorations of Oak Island by Rick and Marty Lagina, Craig Tester, Dan Blankenship and many other great folks.

Friday 13th, October 1307 – The Knights Templar were dissolved on this day. European members of this financial and military organization are rumored to have joined with other Knights Templar in Scotland, fading into Scottish clans or into other groups, particularly the stonemason guilds, which gave birth to the Freemasons. Several Templar properties are granted directly to clans who later include Baronets of Nova Scotia, and who also provide some of the very first Freemasons in history.

Also, the de Sudeley family of England, reported keepers of the famed Ark of the Covenant and/or other Christian relics, possibly makes its escape to Scotland to become the de Suttie family – a family which eventually includes a Baronet of Nova Scotia.

1370 – The Black Death plague hits the British Isles, followed by three more plagues in a row, up until 1401.

1378 – Beginning in this year, through 1417, three men claim to be the true Pope, splitting the Catholic Church.

1384 – Beginning in this year, through 1406, four kings rule Scotland, along with a man who rules it as a regent, refusing to ransom the rightful king. Chaos reigns.

1398 – Legend says that Henry Sinclair, of Scotland, sets sail to the west, with other noblemen, to discover if a special land does exist there. Scotland was coping with many serious challenges at the time, and this may have been when the idea of a "New Scotland" began.

1440 – The history of Scotland is collected in a book called the *Scotichronicon*. The original book, and the first transcription of this book disappear from Scotland. This book joins the Scottish coronation chair, or Stone of Destiny, as two relics of Scotland that would be desired in a New Scotland, or Nova Scotia, and whose current locations cannot be identified beyond question.

1497 – Just five years after Christopher Columbus stuns the world by "discovering" America, Sebastian Cabot explores, and perhaps even discovers Canada, including the land that would become Nova Scotia.

1541 – Jacques Cartier attempts a settlement at Cape Sable Island, Nova Scotia, or perhaps at St. Croix.

1558 – Nicolo Zeno publishes a book that purports to tell how his forefathers helped a Scottish prince reach North America in the 1390s. That prince is said, by some, to be Sir Henry Sinclair, and it is claimed he made it to the land that would become Nova Scotia.

1567 – James, son of Mary, Queen of Scots, becomes James VI of Scotland, and will one day become James I of England and Ireland, as well. Sir William Alexander, who plays a central role in our story, is born in Scotland into a branch of the powerful Clan Donald, in this year, although other records perhaps mistakenly give 1576 for his birth. He becomes a tutor for Charles, son of James VI of Scotland, James I of England and Ireland.

1603 – James VI inherits the throne of Queen Elizabeth of England and Ireland and moves to England, taking William Alexander with him. Alexander publishes his first book in this year. The new King James I grants knighthood to Sir Francis Bacon.

1604 – Bacon is appointed as the King's "Council." Also, in this same year, five French ships sail into the mouth of the St. Croix River and establish a settlement on a small island which they named Île Ste.-Croix. This is the beginning of a permanent French presence in North America. Among those who arrive, in 1604, is Samuel de Champlain, who makes extensive records of Nova Scotia, which the French have named Acadia.

1605 – These same Frenchmen leave Île Ste.-Croix, and establish a settlement in Acadia (Nova Scotia) called Port Royal. Over two hundred years later a stone is found there with the date 1606 chiseled on it.

1609 – William Alexander is knighted by King James.

1613 - Port Royal is attacked by the English Captain Samuel Argall, and the French fort is removed, though many French settlers remain in the area as farmers.

1614 – Sir William Alexander is appointed "Master of Requests" for Scotland, overseeing all requests made to the Privy Council, or cabinet of the king, thus giving him considerable control over Privy Council matters.

1615 – Sir William Alexander is made a member of the king's Privy Council.

1616 – Sir Francis Bacon is made a member of the king's Privy Council.

1618 – Bacon is named Lord Chancellor of England.

1620 - The famous Plymouth Colony is established in Massachusetts and Puritans there complain to King James about French Catholics living to the north. The king asks for advice from Sir William Alexander who then proposes the establishment of a New Scotland in Acadia.

1621 – On September 10, 1621, King James I signs a grant in favor of Sir William Alexander covering all of the lands "between our Colonies of New England and Newfoundland, to be known as New Scotland." In the Latin charter, New Scotland is written as Nova Scotia, and this name has been applied to this land ever since.

Also, in 1621, due to charges made by his political enemies, Sir Francis Bacon is arrested and spends a short time in prison until he is freed by King James. This is the end of his political career, although he continues to write books and make new discoveries.

1622 - Sir William Alexander sends a ship to explore Nova Scotia. This ship is blown back to Newfoundland where many of its crew remain until the following year.

1623 – A second ship is sent to rescue the crew from the 1622 ship, but only ten men are found. They join with this ship to explore the coast of Nova Scotia, returning to England with a positive report, which Sir William uses in advertisements for settlers to go to Nova Scotia.

1624 - The idea of establishing the Baronets of Nova Scotia to create a utopia in this land to the west is devised by Sir William Alexander and King James. In that same year, Sir Francis Bacon begins to write a book called *New Atlantis*, which deals with the establishment of a utopia to the west, only he places his utopia in the Pacific Ocean. On October 18, 1624, the king announces his intention to create a new order of baronets for Scottish "knichts and gentlemen of cheife respect for the birth, place, or fortounes."

1625 – James dies on March 27, 1625. Four days earlier the final adjustments to the Baronets scheme were made, but the king never got to see the plan underway. His heir, Charles I, loses no time in implementing his father's plan. By the end of 1625, the first 22 Baronets of Nova Scotia are created and, as inducements to settlement of his new colony of Nova Scotia, Sir William Alexander offers tracts of land totalling 11,520 acres "to all such principal knichts & esquires as will be pleased to be undertakers of the said plantations & who will promise to set forth 6 men, artificers or laborers, sufficiently armed, apparelled & victualled for 2 yrs." More adjustments are made to the plan, and eventually about 120 men sign on.

Also, in 1625, according to one Alexander family genealogy, John Alexander is born in Nova Scotia, being the son of John Alexander, and the grandson of Sir William Alexander. This puts the Alexander family in Nova Scotia before the first ships of Baronet settlers leave for Nova Scotia. The younger John is said to have been born "on the Alexander estate," in Nova Scotia. He lived there at least until 1650 when his son, Alexander Alexander, was born at New Ross. He left probably around 1654, as Oliver Cromwell was making his move for Nova Scotia. John died in the American colonies in 1677.

1626 – Sir Francis Bacon dies on April 9th of this year while conducting experiments on freezing meat for its preservation, and catching a cold in the early spring weather. This same April sees a mention of David Alexander as the master of the ship *James*. That summer, William Alexander Sr. begins making his plans for an expedition fleet to be sent to Nova Scotia carrying permanent settlers.

Also, in this year, the official Coat of Arms for Nova Scotia is established, and William Alexander Jr. appears to already be living in Nova Scotia. Anthony Alexander is sent to Europe in 1626, for a three year period, "the better to qualify him for gaining of languages and for otherwise doing his Majestie and his countrie service." This includes the study of European architecture, which sets Anthony up to later be named Master of Works for Scotland, and to become one of the first Freemasons.

1627 - On April 2, 1627, the king writes his exchequer asking him to carry on with the appointment of David Alexander as "Chieffe Work Maister for fortifications within our kingdome..." Also, under David Alexander, the ship *Alexander* takes two French ships on her very first voyage in 1627, and shortly thereafter, David takes a ship from Holland laden with "ore."

Meanwhile, Sir William Alexander Sr. and Baronet Archibald Acheson are named "conjunct" Secretary of State, as William Sr. also attempts to get his fleet of ships ready for the first trip to Nova Scotia, carrying permanent Port Royal settlers, under his son's command.

William Sr. is named Admiral of Nova Scotia, with David Kirk, one of the five Kirk brothers, named as his Vice-Admiral. In 1627, Kirk captures 18 French ships, with 135 pieces of ordinance (cannons) whose destination was Nova Scotia and Quebec. This leads to several new members of the Baronets of Nova Scotia signing on to the program.

1628 – William Alexander Jr. accepts the role as leader of the Port Royal Scots, is knighted by the king, as Knight Admiral of New Scotland, and prepares to take the reigns of the whole enterprise. Based on a variety of sources, it appears the *Eagle* leaves London around March 28th to meet up with the *Morning Star*, still harbored in Dumbarton, Scotland. Along the way they are joined by the *Alexander* and the *James*, to make their final launch from the British Isles at the Isle of Man, in August of 1628, taking six weeks to reach Newfoundland.

In mid-September 1628, William Alexander Jr.'s small fleet is blown back to Newfoundland by a storm, where the settlers are set ashore to spend the winter. William Jr. heads back to Great Britain for more supplies.

In November 1628, Anthony Alexander is set to be appointed as co-Master of Works along with James Murray, who had held that position for the last few years, and who appears to have been planning on retirement.

In December 1628, William Alexander Sr. is granted the sole right to the printing of *The Psalms of King David, translated by King James,* much of which Sir William had actually translated, himself.

Also, at the end of 1628, the poet Robert Haymen writes a fairly long poem about Sir William Alexander Sr., which ends with the lines – "Old Scotland you made happy by your birth, New Scotland you will make a happy earth," showing that Alexander's venture is looked upon as creating a utopia.

Just the year before, Sir Francis Bacon's book *New Atlantis,* about the creation of a utopia to the west, was finally (and posthumously) published. With William Sr. having exclusive rights to publish King James' work posthumously, could it be that he likewise saw to it that Sir Francis Bacon's book on creating a utopia was also published posthumously, just at the time he was undertaking such a utopian project?

1629 – William Alexander Jr. finally arrives in Port Royal in the summer of 1629. The Mi'kmaq easily enter into an agreement with the Scots and Chief Sagamore

Segipt accepts leadership of the various First Nation branches, and agrees to go to London as a representative of all Native people in Nova Scotia. It appears, from genetic study and naming patterns, that William Jr. had a child with Segipt's daughter, who was then named Daniel LeBlanc – Daniel being the name of the ship's captain who took Segipt to Great Britain, and LeBlanc, because of the child's white skin.

In January of 1629, a statement is laid before the English government, which read: "The King of France, by his commissions, doeth assure to himself all that part of America... whereby he doeth incluid the River of Canada, all Acady (Acadia), etc."

On April 23, 1629, a treaty of peace is signed between France and England in which it is provided that, though prizes taken during the war should be retained by the captors, whatever was seized on either side, for two months after the signing of the peace, should be restored. In their minds, Port Royal belonged to the French according to the treaty. Not so, with William Alexander.

Also, in the autumn of 1629, Claude de la Tour, former leader of the French at Port Royal, returns there after marrying an Alexander-related woman in England, and after accepting an honorary Baronet of Nova Scotia land grant extending 30 to 40 miles inland from Yarmouth to Lunenburg.

1630 - In February, the English government sends a note asking that "Sir William Alexander, and certain others... withdraw themselves therefrom, and restore into the hands (of the King of France)... all places and spots which they have occupied and inhabited since the last troubles, and in particular... Quebec, the Coast of Cape Breton, and Port Royal."

On April 20, 1630, King Charles I names Anthony Alexander and James Murray as co-Master of Works for Scotland. The actual appointment reads:

Master Of Work To The Crown Of Scotland
Grant by King Charles I to
James Murray of Kilbabertoun and Anthonie Alexander.
Given at Whitehall, April 20, 1630.

Ane lettre maid be our soverane lord... to and in favouris of his hienes lovittis and Servitouris James Murray of Kilbabertoun and Anthonie Alexander sone lawfull to his hienes trustie and familliar counsallor Sir William Alexander of Menstrie, Knicht, his hienes secretare of the said kingdom of Scotland, generall surveyaris and principal maisteris of his hienes werkis and buildinges within the said realme of Scotland...

There is at least the chance that Anthony Alexander was named as a co-Master of Works along with the son of the previous Master of Works in an attempt by Charles to soften the blow of the possibility that the Port Royal Scots, led by the Alexander family, would soon need to leave Nova Scotia. Oddly enough, on April 29, 1630, the Privy Council assured the Baronets, by royal letter, that the settlement of New Scotland is still underway. That autumn, William Jr. returns to Great Britain, leaving Sir George Home in charge of the Port Royal Scots.

1631 – On July 10, 1631, William Alexander Sr. is finally told to abandon Port Royal, in a letter from Charles I, which reads, in part,

Wheras ther is a finall agreement made betwixt we and our good brother the French King... we have condescended that Port Poyal shall be putt in the estate it was before the beginning of the late warre... we command yow to give ordour to Sir George Home, Knycht, to demolish the fort which was builded by your Sone there, and to remove all the people, goods, ordinacnes, munitions...(etc.) this yow faill not to doe, as you wil be answeable unto us.

Charles was vacillating on this issue, as he, just two days later, on July 12, 1631, assured the Privy Council that he was resolved to maintain the colony at Port Royal. Whether he was simply being indecisive, or actually didn't even realize what he was signing, is questionable, as he later wrote that he did not understand that the abandonment of Port Royal was included in the treaty with France, and he continued to issue charters for Baronets of Nova Scotia until 1638, which included a land grant.

On July 28, 1631, the Privy Council issues a statement to the Baronets that "so farre from quitting his title to New Scotland, (his Majesty) will be verie carefull to maintean all his good subjects who doe plant thameselfis there."

Confusion seems to surround the whole issue, and though Scots in Port Royal are made aware they may need to leave at some point, no movement is being made towards that end.

Meanwhile, in 1631, specific evacuation orders are sent to the French in Quebec, to be enacted upon at the very beginning of the following year.

1632 – At this point in British history, a new year began on March 25th. It appears that around March 25, 1632, three hundred French soldiers left Quebec and descended upon Port Royal demanding that the Scots fort be torn down, and giving the Scots eight days to gather their belongings (including gold and silver), and three additional weeks to set sail.

This would mean that on or about April 27, 1632, the Port Royal Scots would have rounded the cape of Nova Scotia to potentially face an angry ocean, based on weather reports representing typical North Atlantic sailing conditions in late April, early May.

It is my contention that this small fleet of heavily laden Scots ships took refuge in Mahone Bay, due to gale force winds, freezing spray, and seas of up to 15 feet. The most obvious choice of the 350 or more Mahone Bay islands to find shelter at would have been Oak Island, since a direct wind tack from the ocean leads there, and the waters around the island were deep enough to anchor ships.

Also, I believe that one of their ships either wrecked in the area that is now known as the swamp, or was purposely scuttled there, either because it was too damaged to continue the voyage, or because they did not want its existence, or the cargo it contained to be discovered. A dam was then built to retain the ship and its cargo within the area that became the swamp.

As carbon-dating evidence allows for, it is entirely possible the Scots remained on Oak Island for at least a couple of months, burying other items in the Money Pit, and perhaps elsewhere. Their leader, Sir George Home, may have stayed behind, along with Claude de la Tour and his Alexander-related wife, as well as John Alexander, grandson to William Sr. (John was born in Nova Scotia in 1625, and, at some point, began living at the area that would become New Ross).

In mid-June of 1632, the king and other interested parties in Great Britain are told that the Scots had abandoned Port Royal.

1633 – Oddly, in this year William Alexander receives a commission from Charles I to continue his enterprise in Nova Scotia, along with issuing Baronet titles, which included land grants that are chartered until 1638.

July 3, 1634 – The first three Freemasons in history are initiated into a stonemason's lodge in Edinburgh, Scotland. They are listed in order as William Alexander Jr., Anthony Alexander, and Sir Alexander Strachan, a Baronet of Nova Scotia.

Anthony is admitted to quash complaints by William Sinclair that Anthony was not engaged in any of the building trades, and yet had been named Master of Works of Scotland, a position that oversaw all major royal building construction and repair. Why, exactly, he was joined by his brother William, and by Alexander Strachan is yet to be discovered, unless they felt there was safety in numbers, since they would be entering as the very first non-operative, speculative Freemasons – an entity which did not exist until that very day.

Over the next few years, these men may have imparted knowledge about the design of the Money Pit that then became immersed in Freemason ritual until the actual Money Pit was discovered.

1635 – John Alexander is, conjointly with his father, Sir William Alexander, appointed co-Master of Minerals and Metals in Scotland. It would seem that John must have been in Nova Scotia as early as 1625, for his own son John to have been born there in that year.

1636 – A lot takes place in this year. The Alexander family's French ally, Claude de la Tour, dies in or just after 1636, in Nova Scotia. Sir George Home, leader of the Port Royal Scots in the absence of William Alexander Jr., is said to have died in or around 1636, and there is at least a chance he also died in Nova Scotia. Agnes, wife of the above mentioned John Alexander, also dies, at a young age, in 1636. This year seems to kick off a series of strange deaths related to the Alexander family.

1637 – Anthony Alexander dies in this year, at the young age of 47, and just three days after he wins the final battle with William Sinclair over his position as Master of Works for Scotland. Obviously, his death was unexpected, or such a political battle would never have been fought to gain him this title.

Anthony was married to the daughter of Sir Henry Wardlaw, another Baronet of Nova Scotia, who owned 16,000 acres there called the Barony of Wardlaw, and who also dies in 1637, the same year as his son-in-law!

Anthony is followed immediately, as Master of Works, by his brother Henry.

1638 – This year marks the end to Baronet titles being sold with the inclusion of a land grant. It also marks the year that William Alexander Jr., leader of the Baronet adventure in Nova Scotia dies at the young age of 34, possibly while in Nova Scotia (as some Alexander genealogy records say).

That same year, 1638, another Alexander brother (Robert) dies at age 25.

The significance of this cannot be overstated. Two of the first Freemasons in history died just one year apart, at ages 47 and 34, along with another brother at age 25. They were not only brothers, but men who were closely tied to the Baronet of Nova Scotia venture.

Another brother, Sir Henry Alexander, joins the Freemasons in 1638, most likely because he inherited the position of Master of Works from his deceased brother Anthony. Unlike Anthony, Henry had not been sent to study European architecture, and had no real training that would have qualified him. He remains in this position until 1641, and dies in 1647, as some records say, or perhaps in 1645, as others state. Either way, he'd have been only 40 to 42-years-old, again too young to die, especially when all the other deaths are factored in.

1639 - The Bishops' Wars were conflicts, both political and military, which occurred in 1639 and 1640, centered on the nature of the governance of the Church of Scotland, and the rights and powers of the Crown. They are the forerunner to a larger political conflict across Scotland, England and Ireland, and are often considered a prelude to the English Civil Wars that saw Charles I beheaded, and Oliver Cromwell taking over most of the British Empire as a sort of secular leader, rather than an ordained king.

1640 – Two more Alexander family deaths take place in this year. Sir William Alexander Sr. dies heavily in debt, as his debtors surround his deathbed, giving him no peace until his passing on September 12, 1640. The "British" son of William Alexander Jr. was also named William. This very young William III also dies in 1640, just three months after being named Lord Stirling.

1641 – John Alexander leaves his position as General of the Mint, in this year, and his brother Henry leaves his position as Master of Works. It appears that perhaps without the powerful influence of their now-deceased father, their political power was waning. It was also in this year that Robert Moray became a Freemason. A son and grandson of a Baronet of Nova Scotia, Moray later co-established the Royal Society along with another son of a Baronet. In 1665, Moray gave a lecture at the Royal Society on how a specially designed, charcoal-fired furnace, located at 30 feet below ground, could bring oxygen to those working below this level. As the Oak Island Money Pit was being uncovered, over a century later, charcoal was found at the 30-foot level.

1642 – John Alexander, former General of the Mint, dies perhaps in Nova Scotia. Alexander family records say he had a son, also named John, who was born in Nova Scotia in 1625, and who lived at New Ross when his own son, Alexander Alexander, was born there in 1650.

1645 – Date given for the death of Henry, at age 45.

1647 – This alternative date is more typically given for the death of Henry Alexander, at age 47. This would seem to be the last of many mysterious deaths occurring from 1636 through 1647, involving people closely associated with the Scots settlement at Port Royal, under the auspices of the Baronets of Nova Scotia, and their leaders, the Alexander family, although two other brothers die later at relatively young ages of 52 and 55.

1649 – Charles I is beheaded by the forces of Oliver Cromwell, and perhaps the last real link to the Scots settlement at Port Royal is gone. Cromwell also begins his attacks on rebels in Ireland, in this year.

1650 - Cromwell begins attacks on forces in Scotland in this year, eventually bringing all of Great Britain under his control. Next, he eyes Nova Scotia.

1651 – David Alexander is captured by the forces of Oliver Cromwell.

1654 – Cromwell acknowledges Charles de la Tour's inheritance of Nova Scotia from his father, Claude de la Tour, ally of the Alexander family. Charles de la Tour immediately sells his rights to two Englishmen for enough money to pay off his debts. This puts Nova Scotia ostensibly in the hands of Great Britain, although battles for this land continue unabated for many years to come.

1733 – The last claim on Baronet land is settled with Agatha Campbell, granddaughter of Charles de la Tour.

1795 – The Money Pit on Oak Island is found. Successive treasure hunters and investors help explore the island, many of whom are Freemasons. But just what was left behind on Oak Island, perhaps in 1632, and where does it lie today? This is the burning question that has been asked for 222 years.

The mainland around Oak Island slowly became populated, first by the French, and later by people from Great Britain – a considerable number coming from Scotland, and Nova Scotia is, today, often referred to as being "more Scottish than Scotland."

It seems that the dream of creating a New Scotland, or Nova Scotia, held by William Alexander, and perhaps by Henry Sinclair, did indeed finally come true.

Sir William Alexander, founder of the Baronets of Nova Scotia,
Secretary of State, and member of the Privy Council of King James I.

EPILOGUE

The reconstruction of historical events can be a risky business. However, in the case of *Oak Island 1632* there was a wealth of documentation available to be weaved into a reasonable and pragmatic theory on Oak Island.

As I said with my first book, *Oak Island Missing Links*, this book will have its share of fans and doubters.

It is not for me to worry about them, but only to report what I have found, based on my many years experience in researching and writing about Scottish clan history, and my long fascination with the mysteries of Oak Island. If my research helps the current Oak Island treasure hunters, then I've done my job.

I thank all of those, over many years, who have helped me understand Scottish history, who have supported my writing efforts, and who have believed in my ability to dig mysteries down to their often pragmatic, yet heroic roots.

I'd also like to thank my wife, Beth, for her patience, encouragement, and excellent proofreading efforts, and to thank the folks currently chasing the Oak Island mystery for their encouragement to pursue this book, and my previous book.

I wish them great success.

MORE BOOKS BY THIS AUTHOR

I have published several non-fiction books on lesser-known historical figures, plus one historical fiction work in the same vein. All are available on Amazon.com and other online bookstores. These include:

Oak Island Missing Links – A look at the various legends surrounding Oak Island, Nova Scotia, with some plausible explanations. This was the forerunner to the book *Oak Island 1632*.

Captain Jack: Father of the Yukon – The story of the first 25 years before the Klondike Gold Rush, and the man who led the way, earning, in his own lifetime, the monikers of "Father of the Yukon," "Father of Alaska," "Injun Papa," and "Yukon Jack."

Ebenezer Denny: First Mayor of Pittsburgh – The story of a man who had already led a full life as a privateer and a Revolutionary War hero, and who wrote the most-often quoted description of the surrender of the British at Yorktown, before becoming the first Mayor of this important frontier town.

Patrick's Run – An historical fiction account of Patrick Fitzpatrick, a hero of the War of 1812, who was wrongfully executed for a crime he didn't commit, thus causing Michigan to become the first English-speaking territory in history to outlaw the death penalty.

McUisdean – A 286-page family history of the McQuiston family and its parent clan, Clan Donald.

The Vatican And The White House – A short historical account of two men who appear to have caused the Vatican and the White House to come together for their mutual benefit, just before and during WWII. This book was originally a report accepted by the Franklin Delano Roosevelt Presidential Library and Museum.

REFERENCE MATERIAL

I've used many resources over the years to understand Scottish history. A few worth mentioning, in regard to my Baronets of Nova Scotia research, are listed here in chronological order, by year of publication. Without a doubt, the most valuable were *The Registry of the Privy Council of Scotland*, *The Origins of Freemasonry*, and the *Memorials of the Earl of Stirling and the House of Alexander*, each of which provided invaluable documentation.

• *The Registry of the Privy Council of Scotland*, those volumes regarding the Baronets of Nova Scotia, and spanning the mid-16th through the mid-17th centuries;

• *Gesta Gragorum*, Sir Francis Bacon, 1594;

• *Works of Samuel de Champlain*, Samuel de Champlain, 1610-18

• *History of the Province of Moray*, Lachlan Shaw, 1775

• *Royal Letters, Charters, and Tracts Relating To The Colonization Of New Scotland And The Institution Of The Order Of The Knights Baronets Of Nova Scotia 1621 – 1638*, The Bannatyne Club, 1827

• *History of the Lodge of Edinburgh*, David Lyon, 1873.

- *Memorials of the Earl of Stirling and of the House of Alexander*, Rev. Charles Rogers, 1877

- *Transaction, Vol. XXXI*, North Of England Institute of Mining and Mechanical Engineers, 1881-82

- *The Gold Fields of Nova Scotia*, Walter H. Prest, 1915

- *The Surnames of Scotland*, George Black, 1946

- *The Vikings*, Frank R. Donovan, 1964

- *The Highland Clans*, Sir Ian Moncreiffe, 1967

- *Cows, Pigs, Wars, and Witches: The Riddles of Culture*, Marvin Harris, 1974

- *Clan Donald*, Donald MacDonald, 1978

- *The Origins of Freemasonry*, David Stevenson, 1988

- *The First Nova Scotian*, Mark Finnan, 1997

- *Oak Island Secrets*, Mark Finnan, 1997

- *The Sinclair Saga*, Mark Finnan, 1999

- *Terror Of The Seas: Scottish Maritime Warfare 1513-1713*, Steve Murdoch, 2010

- *Irresistible North*, Andrea di Robilant, 2011

In addition, I've referenced several magazine articles, websites, and family genealogies, for specific information used to complete both of my Oak Island books –

Oak Island Missing Links and **Oak Island 1632**